100

THINGS TO DO IN
WINSTON-SALEM
BEFORE YOU
DIE

100

THINGS TO DO IN
WINSTON-SALEM
BEFORE YOU
DIE

• •

TINA FIRESHEETS

REEDY PRESS

Library of Congress Control Number: 2022949260

ISBN: 9781681064215

Design by Jill Halpin

All photos were provided by Visit Winston-Salem.

Printed in the United States of America
23 24 25 26 27   5 4 3 2 1

CONTENTS

Preface .... **xiii**

Acknowledgments .... **xv**

Food and Drink

   1. Hit the Moravian Culinary Trail, Starting at Salem Kitchen **2**

   2. Drink In the Town with a Craft Draft Crawl **4**

   3. Break Bread throughout the City.. **6**

   4. Sign Up for Sunday School at Ginger Fox Beverage **8**

   5. Sample North Carolina Craft Beers and Wines **10**

   6. Bottle Some Gin at Sutler's.. **11**

   7. Enjoy a Hot Krispy Kreme at Its Flagship Store.................................... **12**

   8. Indulge at the (Chocolate) Bar... **13**

   9. Eat Authentic Grocery Store Thai **14**

  10. Fill Up at Piedmont Aviation Snack Bar **15**

  11. Dine In at La Botana **16**

  12. Try That Tomato Pie at Mozelle's **17**

  13. Order a Custom Doughnut at Dough-Joe's... **18**

  14. Make Friends and Forge Relationships
      over Fried Green Tomatoes and Okra.. **19**

• •

15. Bite into a Slice of Mission Pizza **20**

16. Relish Coastal Flavors without Driving to the Beach **21**

17. Follow Native Root for Indigenous Cuisine **22**

18. Feed Yourself with Comfort Food at Café Arthur's **23**

19. Weigh In on the Great Hot Dog Debate **24**

20. "Q" Up Some N. C. Classics: BBQ **26**

21. Recapture Your Youth at a Neighborhood Bar **27**

22. Revive Your Soul with Food **28**

23. Save the Pasta for Next Time; Feast on Rotisserie Chicken **29**

24. Become a Regular Where the Staff Know You by Name **30**

25. Meet Friends after Work at the Library Bar **31**

26. Sip a Cup of Joe **32**

Music and Entertainment

27. Find Inspiration at Innovation Quarter **36**

28. Turn Date Night into Play Night at ROAR **37**

29. Spend a Night in an '80s-Themed Arcade Airbnb **38**

30. Do It All at Bailey Park **39**

31. Gather, Listen, and Create at Industry Hill **40**

32. Broaden Your Film Horizons at a/perture cinema **41**

33. Play like a Kid at the Kimpton Cardinal **42**

34. Have Fun While Learning at Kaleidium **43**

• •

35. Eat, Dance, and Shop at the Greek Festival **44**

36. Hear the Oldest Continuous Mixed Wind Ensemble in the Nation **45**

37. Binge on Films at RiverRun International Film Festival **46**

38. Dance and Sway the Night Away
at the Downtown Summer Music Series **47**

39. Watch a Film under the Stars at Reynolda **48**

40. Chill Out at the Big Chill Fundraiser **49**

41. Gear Up for Cycle Racing and Live Music **50**

42. Kick Off Fall with a Classic **51**

43. Taste and Dance Your Way through Latin America **52**

44. Rock Out in the Coal Pit **53**

45. Feel the Holiday Magic at Tanglewood **54**

46. Hang Out at the Art Park **56**

Sports and Recreation

47. Cheer for the Dash and the Disco Turkeys **60**

48. Score Some World-Class Tennis **61**

49. Get Loud at the Madhouse **62**

50. Walk with the Deacons, Groove to the Red Sea of Sound **63**

51. Stroll around Town **64**

52. Ride a Dinosaur **65**

53. Live the Lake Life at Salem Lake **66**

54. Soak In the Views at the Quarry **67**

• •

55. Catch Some Air at the Skate Park **68**

56. Hug a Tree at C. G. Memorial Park **69**

57. Picnic by a Secret Waterfall **70**

Culture and History

58. Spend a Day at Old Salem Museum and Gardens **74**

59. Browse the Arts District **76**

60. See the Last Shell Oil Clamshell **78**

61. Spot the Old Salem Coffee Pot **79**

62. Explore Graylyn Estate **80**

63. Stand at the Site of the Nation's First Fourth of July Celebration **81**

64. Get Spooked with a Haunted Tour of Winston-Salem **82**

65. Brake for a Tour of the Winston Cup Museum **83**

66. Wander Reynolda Museum, Historic House, and Gardens **84**

67. Dig into History at Bethabara Park **86**

68. Nerd Out over the Architecture of Salem Town Hall **87**

69. Marvel at the Architectural Preservation of West End Mill Works **88**

70. Sit in a One-Room Schoolhouse **90**

71. Pause, Learn, and Reflect: Experience Black History **91**

72. Surround Yourself with Art at West Salem Art Hotel **92**

• •

73. Ride through Old Salem in a Horse-Drawn Carriage **93**

74. Tap into Your Creative Side.. **94**

75. Immerse Yourself in Books at Bookmarks... **95**

76. Learn about the Origins of Regional Food at the Horticulture Lab......... **96**

77. Go to Anything at SECCA... **97**

78. Form New Perspectives through Storytelling.. **98**

79. Celebrate and Honor Black Culture and Heritage................................. **99**

80. Expand Your Knowledge of Black Art..**100**

81. Find an Art-O-Mat **101**

82. Take In Everything at the Milton Rhodes Center for the Arts **102**

83. Delve into Global Cultures at the Lam Museum of Anthropology.......**103**

84. Support Black Theater..**104**

85. Walk through the Doors of a Historic Women's Institution...................**105**

86. Sponsor a Seat at the Stained Glass Playhouse **106**

87. Have a "Marvtastic" Time at the N. C. Black Theatre Festival **107**

88. Study Early Southern Decorative Arts..**108**

89. Perch on a Chair at the Sutton Chair Library **110**

90. Rise Early for an Easter Sunrise Service at God's Acre.........................**112**

91. Meet Authors, Hear Them Speak, Buy Their Books **114**

92. Try to Follow Black's Brick Road **115**

• •

Shopping and Fashion

93. Hunt for Something Vintage and Handmade..**118**

94. Go to Reynolda for a Luxe Day Out **119**

95. Stock Up on Regional Items and Vintage Candy
at Mast General Store..**120**

96. Seek Something Unique at Piedmont Craftsmen **121**

97. Soothe Your Body and Soul..**122**

98. Head to the Fairgrounds for Fresh Meats, Produce, and More!............**123**

99. Shop Sustainably at Cobblestone Farmers Market................................**124**

100. Craft a Handmade Holiday List **126**

Activities by Season **128**

Suggested Itineraries **131**

Index **135**

PREFACE

Camel City. Twin City. The City of Arts and Innovation.

Winston-Salem is known by all of these names.

Camel City is linked to its tobacco history and R. J. Reynolds's Camel cigarettes.

Twin City comes from its dual heritage, which dates back to when Winston and Salem were separate cities.

Today, its title as the City of Arts and Innovation reflects what it has become and where it's headed. It's at the epicenter of groundbreaking research in both medicine and engineering through Bowman Gray Center for Medical Education and Wake Forest School of Medicine.

It's a town that supports its dreamers and innovators by making it possible to turn their ideas into business ventures.

And its thriving community of artists, creators, and makers gives Winston-Salem its flourish, its beauty, and its flavor.

I hope that all of these aspects of Winston-Salem are represented in this book. Its long, rich Moravian history is still celebrated through its museums and time-honored traditions. The abundance of art museums and galleries and music venues and events keeps this city entertained throughout the year.

It's impossible to include all that it has to offer. I'm sure that there are places, events, and activities that were missed. But I hope this book only whets your appetite. I hope that it motivates you to want to do and see more.

• •

ACKNOWLEDGMENTS

I couldn't have written this book without the help of friends and colleagues who live, work, eat, and play in Winston-Salem. Their insight and opinions were invaluable. Jeff "Smitty" Smith was the first person I connected with when I started planning the project. He's the author of the long-running "Smitty's Notes," an e-newsletter roundup of all that's going on in Winston. He's a Winston native, community leader, and tireless advocate and cheerleader for the city. In fact, I think of him as "Mr. Winston-Salem."

Much gratitude is also extended to Marcheta Cole Keefer, Director of Marketing and Communications for Visit Winston-Salem. I will always remember our summertime coffee meeting at Louie and Honey's Kitchen, with my son in tow. We talked about all things Winston over savory kimchi scones. She was responsive, eager to help, and so generous with her time and support since that first meeting. I will never forget her warmth and kindness. And, really, I experienced that same warmth, kindness, and generosity of spirit with each encounter throughout writing this book.

I love food. So, of course, my favorite section of this book is the food and drink portion. Longtime restaurateur and restaurant advocate and supporter Mary Haglund was instrumental in helping me craft this section. Her insight and our conversation about the best eats in Winston had me hungry for days.

I hope this book inspires other people to love Winston as much as y'all do.

• •

FOOD
AND DRINK

HIT THE MORAVIAN CULINARY TRAIL,
STARTING AT SALEM KITCHEN

The Moravian influence is seen throughout Winston-Salem in its architecture and institutions like Salem College. It's evident in its traditions, like the annual Easter sunrise service at God's Acre and the summer concerts at Salem Square. But the reach of its food traditions extends beyond the city limits.

It's a delicious challenge, but you can't truly experience the city's history without tasting the best of what it has to offer. Here are three Moravian culinary all-stars that are always in demand:

Moravian cookies. How can such a wafer-thin cookie pack such intense flavor? Though often synonymous with the holidays, they are delicious year-round.

Moravian sugar cakes are also popular holiday treats. Brown sugar. Pure butter. Cinnamon and honey. This combination results in a delectable loaf of holiday heaven.

Chicken pies. The best way to score a truly authentic Moravian chicken pie is through a Moravian church during its chicken pie sales. They differ from chicken potpies in that they're without vegetables or a thick sauce. It's just chicken bathed in its own savory juices and encased in a flaky pie crust. You can also order one anytime from Salem Kitchen.

50 Miller St., 336-722-1155, salemkitchen.com

FIND MORAVIAN COOKIES (IN A VARIETY OF FLAVORS, BUT MORAVIAN SPICE IS THE CLASSIC) AND SUGAR CAKES AT THESE TRADITIONAL BAKERIES

Winkler's Bakery

Located in Old Salem, bakers in period costume offer samples and explain baking techniques. They still use the original wood-fired dome oven that has been in operation since its installation in 1800.
521 S Main St., Old Salem, 336-721-7302, oldsalem.org/winkler

Wilkerson Moravian Bakery

Moravian cookies and sugar cakes have come out of this family-operated bakery for more than a century. It began when Dewey Guy Wilkerson fell in love with Clara Jones at a love feast. Her brothers built a large commercial brick oven, which Dewey used to hone his baking skills.
3443 Robinhood Rd., Ste. P, wilkersonbakery.com

Dewey's Bakery

A household name since 1930, the bakery actually got its start downtown during the Great Depression. Sugar rationing during WWII made it difficult to meet demands, so customers brought their own sugar to help make their cakes. Today, the bakery is known for its Moravian cookies, sugar cakes, and custom cakes.
2876 Reynolda Rd. (Reynolda Manor), 336-724-0559
262 S Stratford Rd. (Thruway Shopping Center), 336-725-8321
deweys.com

Mrs. Hanes' Moravian Cookies

Down the road, in Clemmons, a Winston-Salem suburb, Evva Hanes, a seventh-generation Moravian cookie maker and her husband, Travis, oversee production of their world-famous cookies. Oprah Winfrey named it one of her favorite things in 2010. Visitors can take a tour and even meet the Hanes matriarch herself.
4643 Friedberg Church Rd., 336-764-1402, hanescookies.com

DRINK IN THE TOWN
WITH A CRAFT DRAFT CRAWL

You don't have to do it all at once, or even in one weekend, but create your own walkable "Craft Draft Crawl."

There are nine craft breweries, all within a 1.5-mile radius of each other.

Fiddlin' Fish Brewing Company: Started by two cousins passionate about beer, Fiddlin' Fish is in a converted tobacco warehouse on Trade Street, with a 15-barrel brewhouse and covered patio for events, live music, and games. *772 Trade St. NW, 336-999-8945, fiddlinfish.com*

Foothills Brewing: A Winston-Salem original that got its start downtown on Fourth St., Foothills Brewing expanded to two locations and national distribution. The release of its most famous seasonal favorite, Sexual Chocolate, draws long lines, and much anticipation. *638 W 4th St., 336-777-3348; 3800 Kimwell Dr., 336-997-9484, foothillsbrewing.com*

Hoots Beer Co.: Originally Hoots Roller Mill, huge concrete rollers used to crush grain into flour. Now brewers develop beers representative of the local culture—blue-collar classics with a nod to what's current and what's coming. Taps pour lagers, stouts, and newer styles like wormwood sours and Heather ales. Its satellite location at 701 Trade Street, sits in the heart of the Downtown Arts District. It encompasses three floors, with ample indoor and outdoor seating. *840 Mill Works St., hootspublic.com*

Incendiary Brewing Company

The modern industrial vibes of this taproom also reminds you of what it used to be. Nestled into the historic and restored former Bailey Power Plant, Incendiary's massive outdoor patio space doubles as a live music venue, Coalpit Live. Its namesake hearkens to the days when it was a coal pit that powered the R. J. Reynolds Tobacco Company.
486 N Patterson Ave., #105, 336-893-6714,
incendiarybrewing.com

Joymongers Barrel Hall

They focus on a huge and ever-changing selection of small batch beers poured fresh from the tap. More than 17 beers are served and many are available only in Winston-Salem. (Joymongers has a Greensboro location—its first.)
480 West End Blvd., 336-608-4290, joymongers.com

Radar Brewing Company

Set in Industry Hill, one of the city's newest, hippest downtown districts, Radar's tap menu often includes a rich lineup of Belgium-style light and dark ales and saisons.
216 E 9th St., 336-999-8090, radarbrewingcompany.com

Small Batch Beer Co.

True to its name, Small Batch brews its beers one barrel at a time. It started as a nano brewery, and then grew to include a bar and full restaurant.
241 W 5th St., 336-893-6395, smallbatchws.com

Wise Man Brewing

Three wise men are actually involved in this endeavor—an accountant, lawyer, and Ph.D. chemist. The friends opened their brewery in a historic building, just on the edge of the Downtown Arts District in 2017. They serve 11 different craft brews and ciders.
826 Angelo Bros Ave., 336-725-0008, wisemanbrewing.com

Lesser-Known Beer Co.

As the newest brewery in this lineup, its brewers are focused, detail-oriented, and champions of underrepresented beer styles, ingredients, and processes.
901 S Broad St., lesserknownbeer.com

BREAK BREAD
THROUGHOUT THE CITY

Is there anything that smells as delicious as a good bakery? Or is there anything cozier than sitting in one, while savoring a fresh, still-warm-from-the-oven pastry?

While it's not uncommon to find bakeries well stocked with cookies, cakes, and cupcakes, those with more than a few bread choices and savory options are harder to find.

HERE ARE A FEW BAKERIES YOU'LL WANT TO SPEND TIME IN

Camino Bakery

The mantra here is "food-focused, community-driven." Its name was inspired by owner Cary Clifford's journey on the Camino de Santiago, a pilgrimage in Spain that attracts strangers from around the globe who bond through food and stories. Camino has a reputation for supporting and hiring artists.

Multiple fresh bread options are listed daily. The handcrafted coffee menu feels decadent for daytime—like the elderflower spritzer or cold fashioned—but is the perfect midday pickup.

There are four locations throughout Winston-Salem. caminobakery.com

Bobby Boy Bakeshop

With artisan pastries that are gorgeous enough to grace magazine covers, Bobby Boy Bakeshop offers an array of fresh rustic bread and savory sandwiches with locally sourced ingredients reflective of what's in season. There's no menu online since it changes daily. Follow them on Facebook (facebook.com/bobbyboybakeshop) and Instagram @bobbyboybakeshop.
1100 Reynolda Rd., 336-955-3284, bobbyboybakeshop.com

Louie and Honey's Kitchen

The Amish cinnamon rolls are legendary. They are the kitchen's signature product and are the size of a salad plate. The hand-rolled pop tarts aren't overly iced. With seasonally inspired cakes and pies that are so beautiful, how do you decide on just one slice? And then there are the unexpected delights like moist, subtly spicy kimchi scones.
401 West End Blvd., 336-422-7500, louieandhoneyskitchen.com

SIGN UP
FOR SUNDAY SCHOOL
AT GINGER FOX BEVERAGE

It's like a paint and sip but with cocktails. Cocktail "students" gather at the bar to learn about cocktails and how to make them. Then they get to drink them.

Hosted by Ginger Fox Beverage, a cocktail bar and event plus catering company downtown, class themes range from tropical cocktails to Manhattans and martinis.

The cost includes the class, two full-sized cocktails, a take-home cocktail guide, and light bar snacks. Classes last for one to two hours.

400 W 4th St., gingerfoxbeverage.com

OTHER CRAFT COCKTAIL EXPERIENCES AROUND TOWN

Single Brothers
Intimate space and casual setting, but with a drink list that can go blue collar or high roller. Look for featured mocktails on @singlebrothersbarws.
627 Trade St., NW, facebook.com/singlebrothersbarws

Eastern Standard
Sophisticated space—those white leather couches make you want to sip slowly and savor the moment. Bonus: a separate mocktail list.
1131 Burke St., 336-479-1100, easternstandardws.com

Fair Witness
It's a friendly, neighborhood cocktail bar where drinks are fancy. You feel fancy just looking at their Instagram feed @fairwitnessfancydrinks.
290 4th St. E, 336-607-4185, facebook.com/fairwitnessfancydrinks

Joyner's Bar
A bar with books and cozy reading, sipping nooks.
854 W 4th St., 336-955-1699, joynersws.com

SAMPLE
NORTH CAROLINA
CRAFT BEERS AND WINES

Carolina Vineyards and Hops offers a relaxed atmosphere in its elegant tasting room near Salem College and UNC School of the Arts.

All of its wines, beers, and food are sourced from no farther than 150 miles away. This is your go-to for a well-rounded sip of the Carolinas. The extensive wine menu rotates every few weeks so that oenophiles can sample all of the varietals that the state produces. But that's not all. Big things are in the works.

This Black-owned tasting room will soon offer more of its own wines. Owners Chris and Kellie Megginson have made their own wine for years and will expand their winemaking into creating the city's first urban vineyard. Gateway Vineyards will sprout right in the heart of downtown. Follow its progression on the website.

1111 S Marshall St., Ste. 184, 336-448-1284, carolinasvineyardsandhops.com

BOTTLE SOME GIN
AT SUTLER'S

The Sutler's Gin bottling parties at West End Mill Works aren't as regular as they used to be. Volunteers used to help bottle the product, which is also distilled at West End Mill Works. They gathered twice a month to help wash, dry, fill, cork, and seal the sleek, charcoal-colored ceramic bottles. It had the vibe of a cocktail party, and volunteers' spots were filled within hours of sending the invitation.

Demand for Sutler's has increased so much that a paid bottling crew now does it. But anyone can still help bottle by reaching out to the distiller, Scot Sanborn. Bottling usually occurs Mondays, once or twice monthly, from 9 a.m. until about 2:30 p.m.

840 Mill Works St., 336-565-6006, sutlersspiritco.com

ENJOY A HOT KRISPY KREME
AT ITS FLAGSHIP STORE

It seems like everything in Winston-Salem can be traced back to Old Salem. Even Krispy Kreme doughnuts.

Back in 1937, the Krispy Kreme Doughnut Corporation rented a space in an old warehouse on Main St. and delivered the doughnuts to local grocery stores. When passersby started smelling the hot, yeasty doughnuts from their warehouses, they asked to buy them. Doughnuts were sold straight to customers on the sidewalk during production times.

Since then, yeasty, sugary doughnut lovers worldwide look for the neon "Hot Now" signs at Krispy Kreme locations. Offerings have expanded to include glazed, iced glazed, filled, and even crullers and fritters. Limited edition doughnuts released through the years include one inspired by another N. C. original, Cheerwine, which is filled with Cheerwine-flavored cream.

You can visit the flagship store in Winston-Salem, which is massive and includes a kitchen. Doughnuts are made fresh, round the clock, daily.

Dine-in hours are 6 a.m. to 10 p.m. Sunday to Friday and 6 a.m. to 11 p.m. on Saturday. Drive-through hours are 3 a.m. to 10 p.m. Sunday to Thursday and 3 a.m. to 11 p.m. Friday to Saturday.

259 S Stratford Rd., 336-724-2484, krispykreme.com

INDULGE
AT THE (CHOCOLATE) BAR

Satisfy that chocolate craving at the Black Mountain Chocolate Bar.

The bean-to-bar artisan chocolate factory in Innovation Quarter produces the star ingredient in the desserts and cocktails on the Chocolate Bar's menu.

Behind the scenes, chocolate makers work in small batches to extract the maximum flavor from each bean. And all of the treats—truffles, bars, tarts, cookies, brownies, and biscotti—are made from scratch right in their own kitchen.

Located behind the historic smokestacks of the Bailey Power Plant and down in the Coal Pit, the modern, inviting space is a sophisticated spot to enjoy a decadent dessert and elegant craft cocktail.

Most menu items are chocolate-forward, but there are some cocktails that aren't. Look for special events, such as half-price wine nights or mixology classes.

450 N Patterson Ave., Ste. 110, 336-293-4698, blackmountainchocolate.com

EAT AUTHENTIC
GROCERY STORE THAI

How does the saying go? "IYKYK" (if you know, you know).

One of the most authentic Thai restaurants in the city is nestled inside the Harris Teeter on Cloverdale Avenue. Some locals nickname it "Teeter Thai."

But don't be fooled by the grocery store setting. This isn't a fast-food joint. The small, family-owned Thai Sawatdee has an extensive menu that includes appetizers, soups, salads, curries, rice, and noodle dishes. There's even a page on the menu devoted to Vietnamese pho.

Chef specialties include grilled trout, stir-fried duck, and crispy catfish. Lunch specials come with soup, the main dish, and a spring roll.

2281 Cloverdale Ave., 336-760-4455, thaisawatdee.net

FILL UP
AT PIEDMONT AVIATION SNACK BAR

The best spots are mom-and-pop spots. This little grill opened more than 35 years ago at the Smith Reynolds Airport, serving breakfast and lunch basics: breakfast plates, burgers, hot dogs, and sandwiches. It's open from 7 a.m. to 1:30 p.m. during the week. Saturday lunches are served on occasion. Check their Facebook page (Piedmont Aviation Snack Bar) for announcements.

Prices are reasonable, and the portions of meat on the sandwiches are so generous that they can't be contained within a bun. It's impossible to close the bun on the chicken Philly, and you'll definitely need a fork for the excess that's fallen out of the pulled pork sandwiches. Salads fill every square inch of a to-go container.

When it first opened, it was intended to serve mostly those who worked at the airport. But its reputation grew through word of mouth. Gracious portions, great value, and a friendly staff have all contributed to the reasons why a community of regulars return to this hidden gem.

3820 N Liberty St., 336-767-4173, facebook.com/piedmont-aviation-snack-bar

DINE IN
AT LA BOTANA

The owners of La Botana advise customers that their food is best eaten at the restaurant, straight from the kitchen. They don't advise it for takeout or if you're in a hurry. Their food takes time to prepare.

Go to La Botana if you're ready to experience Mexican food beyond fast tacos and burritos smothered in cheese. Its location in a strip mall, surrounded by chain retailers, seems an unlikely spot for thoughtful, innovative cuisine. But just give it a chance.

The menu changes regularly, but the vegetarian section may include something like a broccoli jicama salad or portobello sopes. Lunch options might be spinach tacos or sushi-grade tilapia fish tacos.

This is fresh Mexican food reflective of the owners' heritage. Their ancestors are from Nuevo Leon, Jalisco, San Luis Potosi, and those influences show up in their food.

1547 Hanes Mall Blvd., 336-768-6588, labotana-ws.com

TRY THAT TOMATO PIE
AT MOZELLE'S

Vibrant, fresh, and savory tomatoes layered with melty, oozy cheese encased in a deep-dish pie shell that's perfectly browned on top. If the South has a flavor, this might be it.

The tomato pie at Mozelle's is so legendary that it's on the catering menu as a whole pie or two dozen minis.

Tomatoes not your thing? It's not the only reason to check out this fresh Southern bistro at the corner of Fourth Street in the West End neighborhood. There's wild-caught American shrimp and creamy grits, fried chicken (locally raised), with peach chutney or gourmet meatloaf (also locally raised meat) with a tomato marmalade.

Attention to detail is evident here. Fresh flowers grace the tables. Fans in the summer and soft lap blankets in colder seasons for outdoor tables make dining comfortable in all seasons.

You are well fed and taken care of at this little neighborhood spot.

878 W 4th St., 336-703-5400, mozelles.com

ORDER A CUSTOM DOUGHNUT
AT DOUGH-JOE'S

The Krispy Kreme Original Glaze is a Winston-Salem classic. But sometimes you have a taste for something more unique. So go to Dough-Joe's Doughnuts and Coffee in Reynolda Village.

Start with a fresh vanilla cake doughnut straight from the fryer, and then drizzle or top it with original and classic flavors. Seasonal favorites include maple pumpkin, key lime, or rosemary and honey glaze. And look for holiday specialties like mini King cakes, Halloween cookies with spooky sprinkles, or gelt-topped Hanukkah cupcakes.

They change regularly, so follow them on social media for weekly offerings. They're on Facebook at Dough-Joe's NC and on Instagram @doughjoesnc.

The small business also donates a portion of sales directly to organizations that work to make food more accessible in the Winston-Salem area.

Reynolda Village Shops and Restaurants
C, 114, 336-842-3254, doughjoesnc.com

MAKE FRIENDS AND FORGE RELATIONSHIPS
OVER FRIED GREEN TOMATOES AND OKRA

It's been said that "friends have been made and relationships forged over a basket of fried green tomatoes and okra" at Sweet Potatoes.

They are indeed that good. Chef and co-owner Stephanie Tyson is a twice nominated James Beard semi-finalist.

The restaurant, which is Black women-owned, has fed the Downtown Arts District with uptown, down-home cooking since 2003.

Start with something like the crunchy fried pork rind basket, with Mambo sauce or collard green dip. Proceed with Slap Yo' Mama Ribs, Miss Ora's Fried Chicken, or Spaghetti with a Drawl—the drawl comes from the creamy Creole sauce with smoked sausage, country ham, and fried chicken tenders.

You will leave full and with heartfelt gratitude.

607 N Trade St., 336-727-4844, sweetpotatoes.ws

BITE INTO A SLICE
OF MISSION PIZZA

People come for the Pizza Napoletana, or Neapolitan pizza. Mission Pizza's wood-fired pizza is cooked in a 900-degree oven, delivering a crispy, pliable crust with a fresh balance of fresh and locally sourced toppings.

But there's more to Mission than pizza. The owners say it's more like an osteria or casual Italian tavern. The rest of the menu highlights wood-fired vegetables and classic Italian dishes like spaghetti al carbonara.

Its following has prompted accolades that include the James Beard Foundation's Semi-Finalist Best Chef Southeast and 50 Top Pizzerias in the US by the 50 Top Pizza organization. You owe it to yourself to see what the fuss is all about.

707 Trade St. NW, 336-893-8217, missionpizzanapoletana.com

RELISH
COASTAL FLAVORS
WITHOUT DRIVING TO THE BEACH

For more than three decades, Forsyth Seafood Market & Cafe has provided fresh seafood for the Triad. Beaufort natives Virginia and Charlie Hardesty were both the children of commercial fishermen who left the salt life for college farther inland. Although they started corporate careers, they also wanted to run their own business. It made sense to go to what they knew: seafood.

They launched their seafood business in 1984, peddling shrimp from the back of a truck. That business eventually grew into a brick-and-mortar fresh seafood market and restaurant.

Since Charlie's passing, Virginia and their daughter, Ashley Hardesty Armstrong, run the business. Their menu of fresh catches includes crab cakes, clam strips, croaker, whiting, flounder, tilapia, and catfish.

108 N Martin Luther King Jr. Dr., 336-748-0793, forsythseafood.com

FOLLOW NATIVE ROOT
FOR INDIGENOUS CUISINE

The global meets local cuisine delivered by Native Root comes to farmers markets, breweries, and pubs regularly in the form of street food pop-ups. These menus might feature short rib shawarmas, bulgogi banh mi sandwiches, or fry bread sammies with pork belly.

On the other hand, supper club experiences are multi-course, sit-down meals. A starter dish might be a summer succotash with herbed butter and crispy sweet potato, and it may conclude with something like corn sorbet with puffed sweet corn.

Chef Jordan Rainbolt's dishes are inspired by her Indigenous heritage, her training in South Korea, and her international travels. Her food is centered on Indigenous ingredients from the Southeast, which are locally sourced and humanely raised. Her fan base grows with each pop-up and supper club gathering.

Keep updated on where she's serving by checking her website, or follow her on social media @native.root.

native-root.com

FEED YOURSELF WITH COMFORT FOOD
AT CAFÉ ARTHUR'S

If you're looking for comfort food for a comfortable price, go to Café Arthur's.

Unpretentious, with a diner vibe, this is one of those local institutions that attracts retirees, Baptist hospital shift workers, and residents around the Ardmore neighborhood. In fact, if you show up around the time the third-shift hospital staff clocks out, you might encounter a bit of a rush.

Get your fill of a bottomless cup of coffee or a BLT.

If you're feeling fancy, try a golden fried flounder platter or splurge on a 10 oz. ribeye.

They also make homemade pies here. Get the strawberry rhubarb.

1416 S Hawthorne Rd., 336-725-4548, cafearthurs.org

WEIGH IN
ON THE GREAT HOT DOG DEBATE

Who's got the best dogs in town? These local spots cover all corners of the city, and enthusiasts are loyal to their favorites: Pulliam's, Hot Dog City, Kermit's, or P. B's.

The restaurants do serve other items, like burgers and barbecue. But their hot dog following is strong. Join the conversation and give them all a try.

TIP

Be prepared to pay with cash. Some of the restaurants don't accept cards. Call ahead to be sure.

Pulliam's

You can count on them. They've been in business since 1910. The formula, also remains unchanged: buttery toasted buns, red hot dogs, and a generous helping of finely chopped, creamy white slaw.

4400 Old Walkertown Rd., 336-767-2211, pulliamshotdogsnc.com

Hot Dog City

They've got all the dogs here. The basics are beef hot dogs, either 1/4 lb. or 1/2 lb. But you can also get a beef foot-long, beef corn dog, or a veggie dog.

2300 N Patterson Ave., 336-722-8600

Kermit's Hot Dog House

A classic drive-in that's fed the Triad since 1966. This is a whole experience. A waitress takes your order at the car, and in no time, you're devouring the whole deliciously messy order, wishing you'd asked for extra napkins.

2220 Thomasville Rd., 336-788-9945

P. B.'s Takeout

Serving Winston since 1987, this lunchtime staple serves their dogs grilled and in a buttered and toasted bun. They're also served the only way that some Southerners will order their hot dogs—"all the way." That means with mustard, chili, slaw, and onions.

1412 S Hawthorne Rd., 336-748-8990

"Q" UP
SOME N. C. CLASSICS: BBQ

N. C.-style barbecue is typically chopped pork and brushed
with a vinegar-spiced sauce as it's cooking. It may come with
ketchup-based sauce on the side when ready to serve. Barbecue
lovers also are loyal to their favorite spots. The list below is just
a sample of what Winston offers.

Mr. Barbecue: Its reputation extends beyond the city and county limits.
Those hickory-smoked pits have made it a barbecue destination since 1962.
Options are chopped, sliced, and chunky. Brisket, ribs, and chicken also
round out the list. For an authentic experience, get the tray. Add golden fried
hushpuppies, vinegary barbecue slaw, and sweet tea.
1381 Peters Creek Pkwy., 336-725-7827, mrbarbecue-nc.com

Honky Tonk Smokehouse: Brisket is king here. This spot serves Texas-
style barbecue in N. C. territory. But their method reflects an East Texas style,
which is similar to N. C. practices. Hickory-smoked all night long to produce
meat so tender, it fallsoff the bone. It's served on a bun or with Texas toast.
Though the menu may throw some Carolina loyalists (jalapeno baked beans,
corn fritters, and cheese curds), there are enough Carolina classics to make
you feel right at home.
145 Jonestown Rd., 336-794-2270, honkytonksmokehouse.com

Camel City BBQ Factory: This is a more modernized take on a barbecue
joint. The menu has the expected pulled pork plates and sandwiches, brisket,
and ribs. But additional items like craft beer, loaded cheese fries, and
smokehouse nachos, give it more of a pub food dining experience. The food
isn't the only draw to Camel City. This is a family or date night destination.
The industrial-style venue is equipped with indoor arcade games and a patio
with outdoor games.
701 Liberty St., 336-306-9999, camelcitybbq.com

RECAPTURE YOUR YOUTH
AT A NEIGHBORHOOD BAR

You won't find groceries at Swaim's Grocery. But you will find craft beers, vinyl records, and toy musical instruments. This small local bar in the Washington Park neighborhood is kid and dog friendly. It's one of those places where the kids who grew up playing on the porch come back to order their first drink when they're old enough.

On the second Tuesday of each month, customers select a toy musical instrument from baskets around the bar and play it. The music that comes from a chorus of rainbow-colored xylophones sounds goofy, chaotic, and incredibly fun.

For an entirely different experience, walk to Monstercade. The dive bar takes you back to your college days when you went to dark bars that smelled like incense or clove cigarettes and ordered drinks called Demon Seed served in a plastic cup. You almost feel cool again.

Swaim's
232 Acadia Ave., 336-725-9696, facebook.com/swaim's
@swaims_grocery

Monstercade
204 W Acadia Ave., 336-893-8591, facebook.com/monstercade
@monstercade_bar

REVIVE YOUR SOUL
WITH FOOD

Sabrina Wingo's team makes soul food that reminds us of dinner at grandmother's house, except a little healthier.

If you're feeling nostalgic for the food you grew up with, head to Taste of the Triad Restaurant. The menu is extensive with options like oxtails, ribs, smoked turkey legs, fish, chicken, and meatloaf that melts in your mouth. Pair them with staple sides like the collards and cabbage mix, yams, pintos, mashed potatoes, or broccoli casserole. Don't skip dessert and do order the sweet tea–lemonade combo.

Taste of the Triad is also more than a restaurant; it supports local artists by giving them a venue to showcase their original artwork, murals, and music. You support the local community when you eat at the restaurant.

4320 Old Walkertown Rd., 336-448-5932, tasteofthetriad.com

SAVE THE PASTA FOR NEXT TIME;
FEAST ON ROTISSERIE CHICKEN

B. L. L. Rotisserie Factory is an Italian restaurant with the usual lineup of pizza, subs, and traditional pastas. The restaurant is so authentic that Italian flows from the mouths of the kitchen staff as easily as pizza dough in their hands. Regulars call it a hidden gem, vouching for the healing properties of the soup and the deliciousness of the Positano salad.

But the rotisserie chicken is the differentiator. It's been said that it's the best chicken in town.

Chickens are cooked until golden and glistening with fresh herbs in a brick-fired rotisserie oven at the restaurant. Rotisserie chicken has its own section on the menu and also plays starring roles in some salads, soups, and sandwiches. Portions are generous, and the chicken is moist and flavorful.

380 Knollwood St., 336-725-7071, bllrotisseriefactorymenu.com

BECOME A REGULAR
WHERE THE STAFF KNOW YOU BY NAME

The Sherwood is one of those neighborhood restaurants where the staff knows its regulars by name and orders. The menu is standard pub food, with a little something for everybody. They have fun here. You can see it in the menu with delightful surprises like the Willie Nelson BBQ, or the Julius Caesar salad, and Once Upon a Time in Mexico, a Spanish rice and chicken entree. Sometimes menu items are inspired by the staff or family members, which makes you feel even more like a part of the family.

This is your home away from home, and the staff and customers who frequent it are neighbors who have become like extended family.

3348 Robinhood Rd., 336-842-3345, thesherwoodnc.com

MEET FRIENDS AFTER WORK
AT THE LIBRARY BAR

If you thought that bookstores with coffee shops were heavenly, then a bar with books in it is next level. Though you probably won't get much reading done.

The historic A. H. Bahnson House that holds the Spring House Restaurant, Kitchen & Bar is a popular restaurant for celebrating special occasions. When built, the two-story English Country style house was part of a block of large homes along West Fifth Street that was known as "Millionaire's Row."

Give yourself something to look forward to midweek with a reservation at the Library Bar. Gather with friends or a date around the wraparound counter or cozy up on the blue velvet lounge. Enjoy handcrafted cocktails concocted with house-made bitters, syrups, fresh juices, and locally grown seasonal ingredients. Nibble on a delectable appetizer and feel like a millionaire for the evening.

450 N Spring St., 336-293-4797, springhousenc.com

SIP
A CUP OF JOE

You don't just go to coffee shops for the coffee. They have their own vibes, and their own communities. Here are three distinctive spots.

Krankie's Coffee: Go for the locally roasted coffee and handcrafted specialties like vegan Vietnamese iced coffee (made with plum-infused coconut milk). The food and beverage menu is unpretentious, yet adventurous, with vegan and gluten-free options. *211 E 3rd St., 336-722-3016, krankiescoffee.com*

Sayso Coffee: Minimalist space. Minimalist website presence. But their single origin coffee and artisan pastries speak for the quality of their beautiful offerings. To see what they're serving, follow them on social media at Facebook at Sayso Coffee, on Instagram @saysocoffee or sign up for their newsletter. *15 Brookstown Ave., saysocoffee.com*

Footnote Coffee & Cocktails: Books and coffee are as good a match as peanut butter and jelly. At Footnote, you can wander around the adjoining Bookmarks bookstore with your made-to-order cappuccino until you need a refill. *634 W 4th St., Ste. #120, 336-602-1087, foothillsbrewing.com/footnote*

MUSIC
AND ENTERTAINMENT

FIND INSPIRATION
AT INNOVATION QUARTER

What was once a tobacco manufacturing hub of old buildings has been transformed into a mecca of 21st-century possibilities.

Innovation Quarter is a unique, culturally diverse, and creatively rich environment. It's a place where Wake Forest University PhDs are engaged in groundbreaking medical research and medical and engineering students are undergoing training. It's where entrepreneurs are bringing their innovative ideas to fruition, creating products and introducing services that will inspire future generations.

And it's a place where the "Live, Work, Play" concept comes to life with its offering of apartments, labs, co-working spaces, retail, restaurants, and watering holes.

Whether you spend your workday or your day off there, it's sure to leave you inspired.

575 Patterson Ave., 336-716-8672, innovationquarter.com

TURN DATE NIGHT INTO PLAY NIGHT
AT ROAR

This social club is a playground for the young at heart, but with a 1920s theme and more elevated experiences, like VIP options.

Test your golf swing on a virtual simulator in the Great Gatsby Golf Club or let the good times roll with boutique bowling.

More virtual games include zombie dodgeball, basketball, soccer, and lacrosse.

Feeling hungry? Dining options include two fine dining restaurants and a food hall with seafood, American, Asian, and Mexican fare. Quench your thirst at the self-serve beer wall.

Also, look for weekly events like Salsa and Sangria, rooftop yoga, and live music.

633 N Liberty St., 336-917-3008, roarws.com

SPEND A NIGHT
IN AN '80S-THEMED ARCADE AIRBNB

You don't need a converted DeLorean to time travel back to the '80s. Just book a night at Wieners & Losers, an '80s arcade museum and '80s-themed bedroom near downtown.

Guests have access to more than 100 arcade machines collected over 25 years. It's the largest privately owned collection on the East Coast, representing the golden age of arcade games. The arcade's greatest hits include *Pac-Man*, *Donkey Kong*, *Frogger*, and *Space Invaders*.

You'll sleep in an '80s-themed bedroom, with an ET night lamp, rock posters, and other vintage '80s memorabilia. There's also a VHS library, and guests have access to every game console ever made from the beginning to CD platforms.

The Airbnb's host, Scott Leftwich, also opens the arcade one Saturday a month by invitation only. Wieners & Losers is a fundraiser to benefit his arcade game restoration projects.

longlivethe80s.com

DO IT ALL
AT BAILEY PARK

Bailey Park is the place to see and be seen. It's a multipurpose gathering spot for anyone and everyone: students, families, young professionals, movers and shakers, and even social activists. It's also been described as an urban oasis.

Head to the lawn for a picnic and a book on your day off, a free yoga class after work, or kick off the weekend with a concert or outdoor movie. There's a regular rotation of food trucks at lunchtime throughout the week, and plenty of tables and chairs for dining at the park.

This public green space also serves as the perfect location for nonprofit events, 5Ks, and other gatherings.

It's fun and many events are free.

445 Patterson Ave., 336-716-8672, innovationquarter.com/bailey-park

GATHER, LISTEN, AND CREATE
AT INDUSTRY HILL

This is where music lovers, beer enthusiasts, and makers gather.

The Ramkat is a two-level, one thousand–person capacity, handicapped-accessible live music venue featuring legendary and emerging artists. The acoustics are really solid and murals by local artists are scattered throughout the space. Unexpected bonus: the bathrooms are clean, well-lit, spacious, and easy to get into and out of.

Get pre- or post-show beers at Radar Brewing Company or Wise Man Brewing.

In addition, spend some time just making stuff or learning how to make stuff at Mixxer. This is a custom-made space for technology nerds, fabricators, and metal heads. It's where welding intersects with electronics, lasers, and software. And for fun, mix in some woodworking, blacksmithing, and sewing. See what you can make.

1375 N Martin Luther King Jr. Dr., 336-265-7362, wsmixxer.org

BROADEN YOUR FILM HORIZONS
AT A/PERTURE CINEMA

Some mainstream movies are shown here, but this is more of an art house cinema. It's even been called a sanctuary for cinema. You take your seat, knowing that you are among fellow worshippers of independent films.

This is where you can check out an obscure documentary, international film, or offbeat Sundance feature, without any of the background chatter around you.

More than 35 percent of a/perture films are directed by women, and more than 30 percent are made by BIPOC filmmakers. Half are US releases; the other half are international. More than 50 countries are represented annually. Films are selected for their power to engage, inform, educate, and inspire.

311 W 4th St., 336-722-8148, aperturecinema.com

PLAY LIKE A KID
AT THE KIMPTON CARDINAL

You can both play like a kid and act like an adult with an overnight stay at the Kimpton Cardinal, Winston-Salem's first boutique hotel. Take in the marble flooring and art deco flourishes and marvel at its transformation.

The hotel is set in a historic building with quite a legacy. Built in 1929, the former Reynolds Building was the home office for the R. J. Reynolds Tobacco Company for nearly a century. It was also the architectural inspiration for New York City's Empire State Building.

Today, hotel guests can relax in lushly designed gathering spaces and dine on French cuisine at the Katharine Brasserie & Bar.

But if all this buttoned-up adulting has you yearning to let loose, there's a special spot for you. The Rec Room is an indoor playground for grown-ups.

There's foosball, ping-pong, bowling, a mini basketball court, shuffleboard, and in the midst of it all—a two-story spiral slide. It's gloriously fun!

51 E 4th St., 336-724-1009, thecardinalhotel.com

HAVE FUN WHILE LEARNING
AT KALEIDIUM

When SciWorks and the Children's Museum merged in 2016, it combined the best of what both offered: art and science-forward activities that encourage learning through play.

Its newest iteration brings a five-story, nearly 70,000-square-foot play space downtown. This is the spot where STEM, arts, and literacy merge to make learning fun.

Nine exhibitions engage visitors of any age and developmental stage through hands-on and open-ended activities. Travel through space, tour the human body, or explore Earth's geography in the Digital Dome. Create an animation or invent sound effects in the Storytelling area. In addition, experience water by controlling a waterfall or sculpting an ice block in the "Wonders of Water" exhibit.

But its crowning glory is a rooftop playground. Go for a spin on cocoon swings or glide down a zip line; Rooftop Adventure appeals to explorers of all ages.

120 W 3rd St., (the corner of 3rd St. and Town Run Ln.), 336-767-6730
kaleideum.org

EAT, DANCE, AND SHOP
AT THE GREEK FESTIVAL

The annual Greek Festival in May, hosted by the Annunciation Greek Orthodox Church, is where you will find the best and most authentic Greek food.

Many wait all year for the mouthwatering gyros, flavorful roasted chicken, and flaky spanakopita. The menu boasts full course meal options, sandwiches, skewers, and sides. Then there are the pastries; they deserve their own category. Baklava and loukoumades (Greek donuts soaked in hot honey syrup) may even rival Krispy Kreme's.

While you're there, tour the church and check out the market. There are usually cookbooks for purchase, so you don't have to wait all year for your favorite Greek dishes. If you need to work off some calories, the traditional Greek dancers usually invite audience members to join them.

435 Keating Dr., 336-765-7145, wsgreekfestival.com

HEAR THE OLDEST CONTINUOUS MIXED WIND ENSEMBLE
IN THE NATION

To attend a Salem Band concert is to witness a musical legacy that predates the city.

The summer concerts in Salem Square are especially magical—beautiful evenings punctuated with colorful sunsets. It's the backdrop for an idyllic setting that's reminiscent of that popular early 20th-century pastime of summer band concerts in the town square.

Established in 1771, Salem Band is an ensemble with roots that can be traced to the arrival of the first Moravian settlers in North Carolina.

Early records show the arrival of trombones in various voices in 1771. Women were finally invited to join the band in the 1930s, and the band's first female director was hired in 2011. Today, its membership of around 70 players integrates multiple generations—from teens to octogenarians.

The summer concerts have been held in Salem Square since the 1920s and are free of charge. In addition to extremely popular summer, fall, winter, and holiday concerts, the band also participates in special events, music festivals, and collaborative concerts.

500 S Church St., 336-413-2180, salemband.org

BINGE ON FILMS
AT RIVERRUN INTERNATIONAL FILM FESTIVAL

This Academy Award–qualifying festival is held annually in April and is one of the premier film events in the Southeast. It showcases a variety of narrative, documentary, student, animated, and short films from all genres.

The breadth of offerings is so impressive, from Hungarian film noir to French comedies, and everything in between. There are also panel discussions and special events with some screenings. Noted filmmakers and special guests travel to share their stories with audiences.

Venues include Bailey Park, Hanesbrands Theatre, SECCA, UNC School of the Arts, and even Red Cinemas in Greensboro.

All festival screenings are reasonably priced, with special matinee pricing for films screened before 5 p.m. Monday through Friday. There are a number of free offerings during each festival, including family and children's events.

301 N Main St., Ste. 2606 (events are held throughout the area)
336-724-1502, riverrunfilm.com

DANCE AND SWAY THE NIGHT AWAY
AT THE DOWNTOWN SUMMER MUSIC SERIES

Summer nights are for relaxing outdoors. They're even more fun with free live music downtown. And there are plenty of opportunities to catch some tunes from late June through the end of August. On these evenings, music fills the air. Couples dance in the street, children play, and friends gather. Some of the businesses remain open a little later and restaurants and food trucks are hoppin'. The vibe is carefree and summery. It feels like one giant exhale at the end of a long week.

There's jazz at Corpening Plaza from 6:30 to 9:30 p.m. on Fridays, and Summer on Liberty concerts from 7 to 10 p.m. Saturdays at 6th and Liberty Streets. Genres include swing rock, R&B, soul, beach, rock, Latin dance, cover bands, and alt country.

Day-of weather updates are posted on Facebook at facebook.com/downtownws.

Corpening Plaza: 1st and Liberty Streets
Summer on Liberty: 6th and Liberty Streets
downtownws.com/music

WATCH A FILM
UNDER THE STARS
AT REYNOLDA

Pack a picnic, grab a blanket or chair, and enjoy a film in the open air on the expansive lawn of Reynolda House. Cinema Under the Stars, hosted by the Reynolda House Museum of American Art, is one of the area's original summer outdoor film series.

Screenings range from classics like *Breakfast at Tiffany's* to more recent blockbusters, such as *The Devil Wears Prada*. When you have such a beautiful setting and the company of friends and family under a starlit sky, any film becomes more magical.

Gates open at 7 p.m., and films begin at dark. If it rains, the movies are shown in the museum's auditorium. Food trucks and a cash bar are on site but keep your own booze at home.

2201 Reynolda Rd., 336-758-5584, reynolda.org

CHILL OUT
AT THE BIG CHILL FUNDRAISER

Do you dream of all-you-can-eat ice cream parties? Then dreams can come true. Think of this as a community-wide ice cream party for a good cause. The annual Big Chill summertime fundraiser at Industry Hill is always held on National Ice Cream Day (every third Sunday in July). Proceeds from the event benefit the Shalom Project, which runs programs to reduce poverty and promote inclusion, compassion, and justice.

The ice cream tasting is provided by teams representing area churches, ice cream shops, and nonprofits serving those in need. Offerings include good old-fashioned hand-dipped ice cream, popsicles, gelato, and ice cream floats (both beer and soda-based). The event also includes live music, food trucks, a kids' area, and local vendors.

100 9th St., theshalomprojectnc.org/thebigchill

GEAR UP
FOR CYCLE RACING AND LIVE MUSIC

Pegged as the "Biggest Party on Two Wheels," the annual Gears and Guitars festival in September is a family-friendly event for anyone.

Organized by Winston-Salem Cycling, it's an entire weekend filled with exciting bike races, community activities, and free live music. Pros and amateurs participate in cycling events that range from drag race–style street sprints to criterium races around city blocks to velodrome competitions. Family fun includes both road and greenway/gravel rides, kids bike rodeos, bike-decorating activities, and a bike parade.

But if you're not into cycling, you don't even need to hop on a bike. Just go as a spectator and enjoy world-class cycle races in a downtown setting. Food trucks and free live concerts are scheduled all weekend.

Friday night events are held on Fourth Street and Saturday and Sunday activities are held at Bailey Park.

475 Patterson Ave., 336-223-5677, winstonsalemcycling.com

KICK OFF FALL
WITH A CLASSIC

Smell that pumpkin spice?

For more than a hundred years, the annual Carolina Classic Fair (formerly the Dixie Classic Fair) unofficially kicks off the fall season. It's held over 10 days, starting at the end of September at the Winston-Salem Fairgrounds. It averages 325,000 visitors each year and features livestock, poultry, and fine arts and crafts exhibits.

There are always the classic things you have to do at a fair, like ride the Ferris wheel or try to win a stuffed animal at a carnival game. Then there are a few things you must experience at the Carolina Classic Fair, like sinking your teeth into a Krispy Kreme burger or wandering over to the butterfly exhibit before hitting the car show.

2825 University Pkwy., 336-727-2236, carolinaclassicfair.com

TASTE AND DANCE
YOUR WAY THROUGH LATIN AMERICA

There are two reasons why you don't want to miss the annual Hispanic League's Fiesta downtown: food and music.

Food offerings may include juicy Mexican tortas and savory birrieria tacos, generously stuffed Venezuelan arepas, golden Chilean empanadas, Dominican slow-cooked pork, and fresh-pressed Salvadoran pupusas. If you're not hungry upon arrival, you will be later. The air sizzles with the aroma of Latin fare.

To burn off some of those calories, hit the dance areas. Music ranges from traditional folk to popular dance music. There are dance performances and contests. Bet you can't resist the urge to salsa.

The Hispanic League has sponsored the festival downtown for more than 30 years. Held in September, it draws an average of 20,000 people, making it the largest one-day Hispanic street festival in the Triad.

336-270-9210, hispanicleague.org

ROCK OUT
IN THE COAL PIT

One of the city's most popular live music venues is staged in a spot that holds great significance in Winston-Salem's history.

Coalpit Live is a free concert series located in the former coal pit where the train offloaded coal for the Bailey Power Plant. The plant powered all of the R. J. Reynolds facilities downtown.

Today, it powers nothing but good vibes. The bustling area is a shared space between a brewery, restaurant, and coffee shop. For Coalpit musicians, it's a great setup because there's already an audience.

Music lovers specifically flock to the area for the concert series that runs from spring through fall. Bands booked range from Eric Gales to the Connells to yacht rock. The roster is also rich with popular local performers.

486 N Patterson Ave., 336-223-5677, facebook.com/coalpitlive

FEEL THE HOLIDAY MAGIC
AT TANGLEWOOD

For more than 30 years, the Festival of Lights at Tanglewood Park has been one of the Triad's most anticipated holiday happenings.

The winding countryside route is aglow with a million twinkling lights from more than 80 displays. Show dates run from early November through January 1.

It's an extremely popular event, and on weekends, expect a minimum two-hour wait to arrive at the main gate entrance to the park. So go early—visitors not inside the park by 11 p.m. may not get to see the show. Pack an in-car picnic and some games to pass the time.

4061 Clemmons Rd., Clemmons
336-703-6400, forsyth.cc/parks/tanglewood/fol

TIPS

To save money, look for discount nights, which are usually early in the week.

Crowds are thinner after December 26. Another way to enjoy it—while burning off some holiday calories—is to participate in the Running of the Lights on New Year's Eve. The event supports a great cause and there are snacks and hot chocolate at the finish line.

Want to make it even more special? Consider these options but book early:

• Horse-drawn carriage rides: To reserve, call 336-766-9540. Cost is in addition to the Festival of Lights admission.

• Tractor-pulled hayrides: To reserve, call 336 766-9540. Cost is in addition to the Festival of Lights admission.

HANG OUT
AT THE ART PARK

Some people call it the Art Park. Or Sculpture Park. Whatever you call it, ARTivity on the Green proves art most definitely belongs in parks. The tall, distinctive red towers and smooth white arches attract people from all age groups and walks of life to this funky area downtown.

The cluster of 13 red towers (known as Tower Cloud) of differing heights mimic the shape of what was once the R. J. Reynolds Building (now the Kimpton Cardinal Hotel).

The bandstand's seven steel ribbons represent the notes of a musical octave. Seating and artist easels are incorporated into the design.

Visit the park for ARTivity After Dark concerts or Arts on Sunday artist festivals. The mural at the park changes each spring during a festival called "Concrete Canvas," where local artists repaint it.

TIPS

Look down after it rains. There are art designs on the sidewalks that can only be seen when they are wet.

The ribbons of the bandstand (those white arches) are also whisper dishes. Grab a friend, sit on opposite seats of the same ribbon, and have a conversation. You can hear each other even at a whisper.

Liberty Street between 6th and 7th Streets, theafasgroup.com

SPORTS
AND RECREATION

CHEER
FOR THE DASH AND
THE DISCO TURKEYS

Isn't summer synonymous with hot dogs and baseball?

Winston-Salem has two teams to support: the Carolina Disco Turkeys and the Winston-Salem Dash.

While the Dash draws larger crowds because they are a Minor League farm team of the Chicago White Sox, the Disco Turkeys (All-American Amateur Baseball Association member) have a fun logo and name. You also may actually hear some disco music during games. They're so cool that Fiddlin' Fish Brewing Company released a fresh new beer in their honor, the Disco Turkey IPA. Their season schedule was even printed on the can.

Truist Stadium
951 Ballpark Way, milb.com/winston-salem/ballpark
discoturkeys.com

FUN FACT
A disco turkey is what folks around the Triad region call peacocks.

SCORE
SOME WORLD-CLASS TENNIS

World-class tennis is served up annually at the Winston-Salem Open. An ATP World Tour 250 Event, it's also the final tournament in a nine-tournament series leading up to the US Open.

Held in August on the campus of Wake Forest University, the weeklong tournament offers a more intimate experience because spectators get the chance to feel closer to the players.

Some have described it as like watching a major-league game in a minor-league stadium. It doesn't draw the very top-ranked players, but it's your chance to preview some rising stars who are on the cusp of becoming household names.

While this is a major sporting event for the city, it's also a significant fundraising effort. The Winston-Salem Open is a charitable nonprofit that benefits middle school athletic programs in Winston-Salem and Forsyth County. It has helped return cross country programs and expand tennis to all of the middle schools in Forsyth County.

Wake Forest Tennis Complex
100 W 32nd St., 336-560-7554, winstonsalemopen.com

GET LOUD
AT THE MADHOUSE

They call it the madhouse.

Every summer, Bowman Gray Stadium thunders with the sound of roaring engines and cheering fans.

It's NASCAR's first and longest running weekly track. Since 1949, crowds have gathered there every Saturday night throughout the spring and summer to watch the races.

The track holds a lot of racing history. Richard Petty won his 100th race at Bowman Gray. It's also where Richard Childress first fell in love with racing, while hawking peanuts in the stands. He later got behind the wheel himself.

A family-friendly event, many pack a picnic for the evening. At the end of the night, the pit area opens to the public, and fans can wait in line to get autographs from their favorite drivers.

All tickets are for general admission seating and are only available on race nights at the ticket booths. Admission is cash only; there are ATM machines at each gate.

1250 S Martin Luther King Jr. Dr., 336-723-1819, bowmangrayracing.com

---

TIP
Since it does get quite loud, ear plugs or noise cancelling headphones are recommended.

WALK WITH THE DEACONS,
GROOVE TO THE RED SEA OF SOUND

Revel in the experience of taking in a big-time ACC football game with the Wake Forest Demon Deacons.

A fan favorite is the pre-game Deacon walk, which is held every home football game. The Deacon Walk begins about two and a half hours before kick-off, starting at the corner of Deacon Boulevard and Piccolo Lane (as in legendary Brian Piccolo, made famous by the movie *Brian's Song*).

This is a procession led by the Deacon mascot, spirit squad, and drumline to give fans a chance to welcome the squad before game time. For more info, visit godeacs.com.

Another can't-miss Winston-Salem football experience is a Winston-Salem State University game. The main attraction is its band, known as the "Red Sea of Sound." The award-winning marching band performs throughout the country and consists of about 145 students, including dancers and drum majors. Their energetic performances always get spectators swaying and grooving on the sidelines. For more info, visit redseaofsound.com or wssurams.com.

STROLL AROUND TOWN

If you like walks in an urban landscape, then here are a couple for you.

The Strollway Pedestrian Bridge is a 1.2-mile route from Fourth Street to the Old Salem Visitors Center and Salem Avenue. It leads though a historic site, reveals the city's beautiful skyline, and connects you with the Salem Creek Greenway.

The path itself features asphalt and crushed-stone surfaces and 12-foot-wide walkways—ample space for both pedestrians and non-motorized bicycles.

Long Branch Trail is a 1.7-mile paved trail through the heart of downtown, parallel to Bailey Park, and along Innovation Quarter.

Highlights include benches, lighting, emergency call boxes, bike racks, bike share stations, and decorative paver areas at major crossing points. Some pavers are made of recycled cobblestones, reclaimed from streets around Innovation Quarter. For a longer trek, it connects to Salem Creek Greenway, which goes all the way to Salem Lake.

Go to the city's website for access points
and to learn about its parks and greenways:
cityofws.org/854/parks-greenways

RIDE A DINOSAUR

Climb on top of a triceratops, spot a dilophosaurus, or get up close and personal with a T-Rex at Washington Park's Dinosaur Playground.

The small, quiet playground sits amidst the Washington Park neighborhood (also known as Southside) and is just a five-minute detour off of I-40. You'll find slides, swings, picnic shelters, a dog park, and plenty of shade. It's super fun for junior paleontologists-in-training and the photo ops abound.

Once you're done here, it's just minutes from Acadia Foods, a family-owned gourmet deli, coffee shop, and market in the neighborhood. Recharge with a cup of Joe or a bite from the deli and maybe even pick up a bottle of wine for later.

341 Park Blvd.

TIP
This park is also another access point to the Salem Creek Greenway.

LIVE THE LAKE LIFE
AT SALEM LAKE

Whether it's kayaking, biking, walking, jogging, or fishing, there's so much to do here. There is a marina, bait shop, and pier at the lake. The park holds restrooms, a picnic shelter, and playground.

The Salem Lake trail stretches almost seven miles, circling around a 365-acre lake. Horses are allowed on it, but not motorized bikes or Segways. The terrain is dirt, gravel, sand, and compressed rock dust. It's this varied landscape—and the wildlife—that keeps the journey interesting.

The trail also connects to the Salem Creek Greenway; so if you start at the lake, you're on a wooded path along a creek, which leads to open green spaces, before delivering you to cityscapes and the Winston-Salem skyline. At the end of it, you will marvel at how one trail can yield so many different views.

1001 Salem Lake Rd.

SOAK IN THE VIEWS
AT THE QUARRY

You go to the Quarry at Grant Park for the views. The focal point is the overlook pier, which extends over the eastern side of the quarry. At the end of it, you can gaze upon the downtown skyline over the horizon, or drink in the deep blue waters of the old quarry below.

This was the site of Piedmont Quarry from the mid-1920s until the early 1970s. When it no longer served as the quarry, it was filled with water.

Once you've absorbed the view, you can admire the locks of love—the collection of padlocks attached to the chain-link fence enclosing the pier.

The park around the pier yields expansive open grassy areas—great for tossing a Frisbee or running around.

Expansion plans for the park include a rock-climbing wall that looks like the quarry, in-ground trampolines, and a 35-foot observation tower with a slide and picnic shelter.

Quarry Park will also be an access point for the Peachtree Greenway and the Waughtown Connector.

1790 Quarry Rd., cityofws.org/facilities/facility/details/quarry-park-97

CATCH SOME AIR
AT THE SKATE PARK

Channel your inner Tony Hawk, or just gawk at the next generation of skateboarders perfecting their arsenal of tricks.

If you know someone who is into skateboarding, take them to Fairgrounds Skate Park, which offers 15,200 square feet of ramps, quarter pipes, grinding rails, bank ramps, and more. It also includes a 325-foot-long "pump" track, with dips and banks to help riders master handling their bikes, skateboards, or Rollerblades. The park accommodates skateboarders of all levels, as well as bikers, Rollerbladers, and roller skaters.

There's a shade structure, water station, and seating area for spectators. It's not staffed, but there is an emergency call station.

Best park perk? Admission is free.

406 Deacon Blvd., Gate 5.
cityofws.org /facilities/facility/details/fairgrounds-skate-park-203

HUG A TREE
AT C. G. MEMORIAL PARK

Hug a tree—or someone else—at C. G. Hill Memorial Park's Ancient Poplar Tree Site.

According to the historical marker at the site, the ancient poplar sprouted there before Columbus sailed for the New World. It grew to a massive height (72 feet tall) and breadth, before it was struck by lightning. Afterwards, it decayed to form a hollow center, which was the perfect place to hide possessions.

A farmer was said to have hidden his cow and calf there from Union Soldiers during the Civil War. It's protected travelers from the rain, and it's also known as "Loving Tree"—a romantic meeting spot for couples.

5600 Balsom Rd., Pfafftown, 336-703-2500, forsyth.cc/parks/CGHill

PICNIC
BY A SECRET WATERFALL

Don't tell anyone. It's a secret.

Or is it?

The secret waterfall at Reynolda Village is a popular picnic and proposal spot.

From Dough Joe's at Reynolda Village, follow the sidewalk to the back of the parking lot. Stay on the road that runs parallel to the soccer field until you come to a path. Cross the bridge and look for the footpath on your left. Listen for the waterfall. That means you're getting closer. You'll eventually come to the most magical hidden gem in the village.

Once there, admire the original rock-faced bridge over the dam that created Lake Katharine on the Reynolda Estate. The dam is made of volcanic rocks found on the estate during construction, and its beauty is still impressive. The bridge was also once the start of a three-and-a-half mile road that looped around Lake Katharine.

2201 Reynolda Rd., 336-758-5584, reynoldavillage.com

TIP

Grab a picnic lunch from one of the
restaurants or shops in Reynolda Village
to enjoy by the water.

CULTURE
AND HISTORY

SPEND A DAY
AT OLD SALEM MUSEUM AND GARDENS

So much of Winston-Salem's history is preserved here. Moravian history. Black history. America's history.

Winston-Salem was settled by Moravians in 1753, missionaries who established an earlier settlement in Bethlehem, Pennsylvania. The nation's first official Independence Day celebration occurred in 1783 in Old Salem (look for the commemorative plaque). Old Salem also houses the state's longest-standing Black church, St. Philips African Moravian Church.

Old Salem's historic district is like a small city within the city that holds a living history museum interpreting the restored Moravian community.

Walk across the iconic Heritage Bridge leading from the Visitor Center to the historic district, and immediately feel transported back in time. Step onto cobblestone streets and see how the Moravians lived and worked by walking through their homes, workshops, churches, and classrooms. You can even sample (and purchase) fresh baked bread and Moravian cookies from Winkler's Bakery, which is still in operation.

At the end of your visit, you will be amazed by all that you have learned.

900 Old Salem Rd., 336-721-7350, oldsalem.org

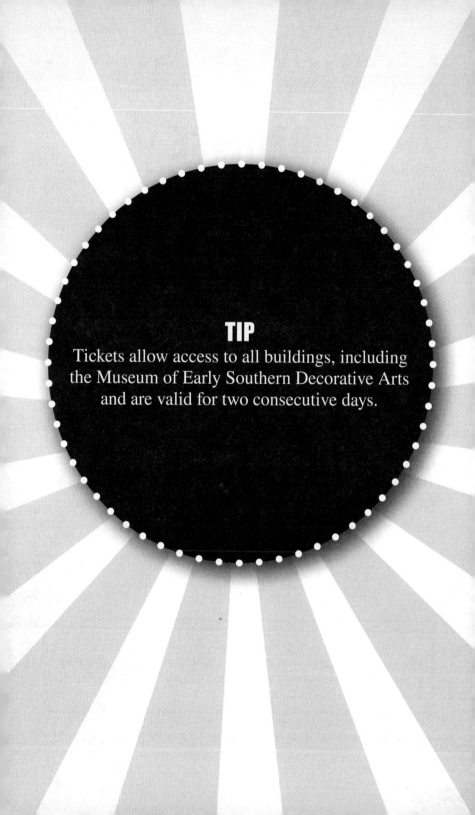

TIP

Tickets allow access to all buildings, including the Museum of Early Southern Decorative Arts and are valid for two consecutive days.

BROWSE
THE ARTS DISTRICT

Trade Street is considered the heart of the city's arts district. Here's how to spend a leisurely day there.

Start with brunch at Sweet Potatoes—try the fried green tomatoes and okra basket or pan-fried chicken. Feeling al fresco? 6th and Vine has a great patio and extensive beverage offerings.

Walk it off by browsing the many galleries and artists' co-ops nearby, including Visual Index, Studio 7, Delurk Gallery, North Trade Street Arts Center, Artworks Gallery, Piedmont Craftsmen Gallery, and Gifted Gallery2.

Shop for shea butter bath and body products or books by Black authors at Body & Soul or stock up on natural beauty and home products at Earth Sage.

Feeling like a happy hour bevvie? Make your last stop the Silver Moon Saloon for a PBR. If you're feeling fancy, go for a handcrafted cocktail—or mocktail—at Single Brothers.

TIP
Be sure to come back for the Downtown Arts District Association First Friday Gallery Hop, along 6th, Trade, and Liberty Streets every first Friday from 7 to 10 p.m.

SOME HIGHLIGHTS OF THE ARTS DISTRICT

Sweet Potatoes
607 Trade St. NW, sweetpotatoes.ws

Visual Index
562 Trade St. NW, visualindex.co

Studio 7
604 Trade St., NW, studio7ws.com

Delurk Gallery
207 W 6th St., delurkgallery.com

North Trade Street Arts Center
604 Trade St. NW, northtradestreetarts.com

Artworks Gallery
564 Trade St. NW, artworks-gallery.org

Piedmont Craftsmen Gallery
601 Trade St. NW, piedmontcraftsmen.org

Gifted Gallery2
619 N Trade St. NW, facebook.com/giftedgallery2

Silver Moon Saloon
632 Trade St. NW, facebook.com/silvermoonsaloon

Single Brothers
627 Trade St. NW, facebook.com/singlebrothers

SEE THE LAST
SHELL OIL CLAMSHELL

Selfie alert: Winston-Salem is home to the last remaining Shell Oil clamshell station in the US.

So here's the backstory: in the 1930s, Quality Oil, a local Shell distributor, built seven stations throughout Winston-Salem.

This last station remained open until the 1950s and has since housed a lawn mower repair business and a regional office for Preservation North Carolina.

It became the first individual station in America listed on the National Register of Historic Places in 1976. Inside, there are framed newspaper articles about its opening, black-and-white photographs, and other clamshell memorabilia.

Preservation North Carolina still holds protective covenants on the property, so this bright landmark will be forever untouched.

The corner of Peachtree and E Sprague Streets.

SPOT THE OLD SALEM
COFFEE POT

It's unlikely that this giant kettle ever held any actual coffee, but at seven feet tall, it has the capacity to hold up to 740 gallons, or about 11,840 cups.

If it reminds you of the Tin Man's oil can from *The Wizard of Oz*, it's because it is, indeed, made of tin. Moravian brothers Julius and Samuel Mickey built it in 1858 to promote their tinsmith shop. It's also been known as the Mickey Coffee Pot.

Many legends surround the coffee pot, including that it provided a hiding place for Civil War soldiers—there are stories claiming it was a hiding place for both Yankee and Confederate soldiers. It's also been said that Moravians drank coffee from it on Easter Sunday, which is unlikely.

Located at the corner of Brookstown Avenue and Main Street, the landmark was often the subject of government debate because it was deemed a distraction and a danger to passing motorists. Traffic accidents have been a common occurrence since horse and buggy days. But the locals love it, so it remains.

wachoviahistoricalsociety.org/old-salem-coffee-pot

EXPLORE
GRAYLYN ESTATE

Imagine a European-style castle that rivals the opulence of Asheville's Biltmore Estate right in the heart of Winston-Salem.

It's known today as Graylyn International Conference Center, but when Bowman and Nathalie Lyons Gray completed their country dream home in 1932, it was the second-largest home in North Carolina, second only to the Biltmore. An avid traveler influenced by the fine homes of the Normandy and Brittany regions of France, Nathalie Gray personally decorated each of the 60 rooms, which total 46,000 square feet.

Now a luxury boutique hotel and conference center owned by Wake Forest University, visitors and guests can tour the home and learn its history or relax and unwind at the spa. Explore the 55-acre grounds on foot, by bike, or borrow a fishing pole to cast a line into the stocked pond on the property.

However you choose to spend the day, make time for an afternoon treat of Mrs. Gray's butterscotch cookies and ice cream, which was Mr. Gray's favorite.

1900 Reynolda Rd., 336-758-2425, graylyn.com

STAND AT THE SITE
OF THE NATION'S FIRST
FOURTH OF JULY CELEBRATION

The circular bronze disc embedded in the bricks of two pathways in Salem Square commemorates the very first official Fourth of July celebration in the US by Salem residents on July 4, 1783.

Just 30 inches in diameter, it also commemorates the year 1966 as the 200th anniversary of Winston-Salem.

Moravian records note that in 1783, North Carolina Governor Alexander Martin declared the Fourth of July to be the day of thanksgiving for the restoration of peace. There was prayer, music, a love feast meal, and even a procession with music through the main street of town.

According to records, "Hearts were filled with the peace of God, evident during the entire day and especially during the procession, and all around there was silence, even the wind being still."

649 S Main St.

GET SPOOKED
WITH A HAUNTED TOUR
OF WINSTON-SALEM

Stroll along the old Victorian streets of the city's West End district and learn about its haunted past, which includes tales of love, greed, and a few unfortunate endings.

Led by Carolina History and Haunts, the 90-minute, candle-lit historical ghost tour reveals ghost stories, superstitions, and quirky tales.

One superstition involves the legacy of R. J. Reynolds, of the Reynolds tobacco empire. The story begins with his great grandfather, Joshua. He believed that his Peruvian coin brought good luck and that it would also bring wealth and luck to any descendant named Joshua.

But if anyone else obtained and tried to use it, then a great curse would fall upon them. The descent of the Reynolds empire seems to coincide with the loss of the coin.

You can hear more about it on the tour, as well as the love story between Van and Johanna Zevely, whose house—now a popular restaurant—is said to be haunted by Johanna.

Tours operate year-round.

Meeting place is 848 W 5th St.
833-628-6277, carolinahistoryandhaunts.com/winston-salem

BRAKE FOR A TOUR
OF THE WINSTON CUP MUSEUM

If you're a racing fan, then the Winston Cup Museum & Special Event Center is definitely on your to-do list.

This spot holds 33 years of Winston Cup Series stock car racing history.

A little background for the uninitiated: The Winston Cup Series started in 1971 when R. J. Reynolds Tobacco Company's Winston Brand became NASCAR's elite division. This ultimately led to what is considered the "modern era" of NASCAR.

The museum is stocked with championship memorabilia, racing artifacts, racing arcade games, and a souvenir shop, making it appealing to seasoned enthusiasts and rookie fans alike.

Best of all, the showroom displays more than 20 authentic race cars, including those driven by Dale Earnhardt, Sr., Jimmy Spencer, and Wendell Scott. To keep it fresh and interesting, every 90 days or so the museum schedules rotating exhibits of personal car collections from all eras.

Every third Saturday of the month, the museum hosts a cruise-in from 10:30 a.m. to 1:30 p.m. It draws between 50 and 60 cars and sometimes includes autograph signings with racing legends.

1355 N Martin Luther King Dr., 336-724-4557, winstoncupmuseum.com

WANDER REYNOLDA
MUSEUM, HISTORIC HOUSE, AND GARDENS

If you love touring grand, historic homes, you won't be disappointed.

The Reynolda House Museum of American Art was originally the home of Katharine Smith and R. J. Reynolds, founder of the R. J. Reynolds Tobacco Company. Their 34,000+ square-foot home on a 1,067-acre estate and model farm was completed in 1917. The 64-room house is now on the National Register of Historic Places and holds more than 6,000 historic objects and a collection of world-renowned American art spanning 250 years. It includes work from artists such as Georgia O'Keeffe, Romare Bearden, John Singer Sargent, Jacob Lawrence, and Andy Warhol.

Special seasonal exhibitions are also displayed in the Babcock Gallery.

Be sure to tour the gardens. The gardens and grounds are a 134-acre outdoor horticultural oasis of lush gardens, scenic walking trails, and a greenhouse that serves as a conservatory. The gardens hosts annual plant sales on the grounds. Become a Friend of the Gardens to get early access.

2250 Reynolda Rd., 888-663-1149, reynolda.org

TIP
Check the website and social media for occasional free admission dates and pop-up events at Reynolda.

DIG INTO HISTORY
AT BETHABARA PARK

Historic Bethabara Park is an archaeological treasure, with more than 40 stabilized archaeological ruins throughout the 183-acre park.

Established in 1753, Bethabara was the first European settlement in the Piedmont of North Carolina. Salem (what we now think of as Old Salem) was established 13 years later. Bethabara was a thriving community with bustling businesses that included a tannery, mill, tavern, and store. There were also cobbler, tailor, and blacksmith shops. A rich mix of archaeological sites and buildings have been restored or reconstructed to their original state.

Trades demonstrations are presented for free at the park throughout the week. They include live blacksmithing, woodworking, textiles, pottery, Colonial medicine, and open-fire cooking demonstrations. They are held outdoors. In case of inclement weather, they move into the outdoor pavilion or barns at the park.

Check the Facebook page for the demonstration schedule: facebook.com/bethabarapark.

2147 Bethabara Rd., 336-924-8191, historicbethabara.org

NERD OUT
OVER THE ARCHITECTURE
OF SALEM TOWN HALL

Here's a gem for architecture nerds and history buffs: Salem Town Hall, Salem's last municipal building before its consolidation with Winston in 1913.

Designed by Willard C. Northup, a prominent local architect, it's the last of Salem's town halls to remain standing. It features both the Italianate style, as well as local Moravian influences.

Once the towns merged, the building served as one of Winston-Salem's main fire stations for more than 50 years. Located at the intersection of South Liberty and Cemetery Streets, it earned its status on the National Register of Historic Places in 1983 and will be forever preserved.

301 S Liberty St.

MARVEL AT THE ARCHITECTURAL PRESERVATION
OF WEST END MILL WORKS

You gotta love a spot where you can knock out several activities all in one stop.

That's what you've got at West End Mill Works. It used to be Hoots Roller Mill Co., a flour mill that served Winston-Salem for much of the 20th century. Today, the gorgeously preserved mill is a testament to how historic architectural preservation can still bring people together.

Here's a place where you can kick some butt at Eight Points Muay Thai, stretch it out with some yoga at the Breathing Room, grab a taco at the Porch Kitchen and Cantina, and then wash it down with a pint and chill at Hoots Roller Bar & Beer Co.

PLACES TO VISIT AT WEST END MILL WORKS

Eight Points Muay Thai
1015 W Northwest Blvd., eightpointsmuaythai.com

The Breathing Room
918 Bridge St., thebreathingroomws.org

Porch Kitchen and Cantina
840 Mill Works St., theporchws.com

Hoots Beer Co.
840 Mill Works St., hootspublic.com

SIT IN
A ONE-ROOM SCHOOLHOUSE

Oak Grove School, built around 1910, served Black children living in the Washington Town community near Bethania from 1910 to 1950.

There were more than 30 public and private schools in Winston-Salem and Forsyth County that educated Black students before integration in the early 1970s.

When Oak Grove closed in 1950, it became a store. Restored in 1998, it now serves as a museum. Beaded board sheathes the walls and ceilings of the original room. Visitors can also browse a small display of desks and teaching materials, along with historical photos and information about the school, its former students, and teachers.

2637 Oak Grove Cir., 336-757-8556

PAUSE, LEARN, AND REFLECT:
EXPERIENCE BLACK HISTORY

Stand on a quiet hilltop of an urban neighborhood and reflect upon the changes that have taken place since its days as a slaveholding Salem farm two centuries ago. Christened "Happy Hill," it became home to newly emancipated men and women, becoming one of the region's first and oldest Black neighborhoods.

This is just one of the many landmarks or sites covered in a Triad Cultural Arts African American Heritage Tour. Destinations also include visits to the former Black business district, historic homes, educational institutions, art galleries, churches, historic graveyards, and the people and places that are shaping local Black culture.

Guided tours are curated for individuals or groups and can be experienced on foot, by trolley, or bus.

336-757-8556, triadculturalarts.org

SURROUND YOURSELF WITH ART
AT WEST SALEM ART HOTEL

Artful lodging. Lodging for art.

That's what you'll experience at West Salem Art Hotel. Stay overnight in one of its two uniquely designed art-partments. Each room—even the bathroom—is designed as a living art gallery, with original works that guests can purchase.

In addition, attend an intimate summer outdoor art film screening. Thoughtfully curated, obscure avant-garde films are selected for discussion and viewing.

If art films aren't your thing, but you do want to support local makers and artists, go to one of the once monthly mini flea markets. They're held Saturdays from 9 a.m. to noon and feature wares from five to six vendors.

The solarium at the hotel is a great place to book intimate celebrations for 20 or fewer guests. Visitors can tour the rooms and gallery spaces inside. Don't miss the opportunity for a tour. Each unique space and wall are filled with art for sale. It's like visiting the inside of an artist's psyche.

910 Albert St., wsarthotel.com
@west_salem_art_hotel

RIDE
THROUGH OLD SALEM
IN A HORSE-DRAWN CARRIAGE

Don't wait for a special occasion—like a wedding—to book a horse-drawn carriage ride.

Heritage Carriages offers 45-minute carriage rides with a narrated tour through Old Salem with a reservation. Holiday carriage rides through Old Salem are magical. Hear the clip-clop of horses' hooves on cobblestone streets and carolers throughout the village. Smell the aroma of Moravian cookies and love feast buns from Winkler's Bakery and take in the candlelit shops and holiday cheer.

If you miss it at Christmas, recreate your own *Bridgerton* experience in a horse-drawn carriage later in the year. Rides are also available for private occasions or events. Note: dashing and eligible bachelors or bachelorettes are not guaranteed.

Carriages comfortably seat four adults and two small children.

3789 High Point Rd., 336-784-8419, thelessonbarn.com

TAP INTO
YOUR CREATIVE SIDE

You're never too old to learn how to create or make something. Sawtooth School for Visual Art is a creative hub that offers online and in-person classes and workshops in 11 visual arts and craft disciplines for youths and adults.

Learn to paint a portrait, turn a wooden bowl, shape a ceramic beer stein, or develop film in a darkroom. All levels of classes are offered from beginning to advanced. Some aspiring artists who took their first art classes here have even returned as instructors.

Go a step further and support other local artists by purchasing original art, jewelry, housewares, ceramics, textiles, and sculpture at the Sawtooth Shop. They make great gifts—for yourself or someone else!

251 N Spruce St., 336-723-7395, sawtooth.org

IMMERSE YOURSELF IN BOOKS
AT BOOKMARKS

Bookmarks is more than an independent downtown bookstore. It's a literary arts nonprofit that aims to unite people of all ages with books and authors. All profits support Bookmarks's outreach programs.

In addition to offering the latest new releases and bestsellers, it's also a meeting spot for book lovers, writers, and aspiring writers. There are also more than 15 community events each month.

The best thing about mingling and perusing the shelves here is that you can treat yourself to a draft beer, glass of wine, or a cup of locally roasted coffee from Footnote Coffee & Cocktails while browsing and connecting.

634 W 4th St., #110, 336-747-1471, bookmarksnc.org

LEARN ABOUT THE ORIGINS OF REGIONAL FOOD
AT THE HORTICULTURE LAB

Horticulturists, hobby gardeners, and anyone interested in the origins of local food can explore the city's harvest heritage at Old Salem's Seed-Saving Lab.

Many of the heirloom crops harvested by 18th-century Moravian settlers are still reaped today, thanks to seed preservation efforts. The lab is located on the second floor of the historic Herbst House on Main Street in Old Salem.

There, in a refrigerator stocked with glass jars, visitors can find 129 different species of flowers and herbs and 37 species of annual food crops. They can even help shell some seed pods of crops, such as cowpeas or okra. Visitors also receive historic seeds to grow at home.

The collection includes crops grown by Native Americans, who lived on the land Salem was built upon, as well as crops sowed by enslaved Africans living or working in Salem.

The seeds are harvested from and sustain the Single Brothers Garden, and since 2020, more than 6,500 pounds of vegetables from Old Salem's Victory Gardens have been donated to area food banks.

900 Old Salem Rd., 336-721-7350, oldsalem.org

GO TO ANYTHING
AT SECCA

The Southeastern Center for Contemporary Art (SECCA) is one of those magical places where you get a lot of art exposure in many diverse forms—fine art, photography, live music, and film—but it never feels unapproachable.

It's not the type of gallery where you feel the need to whisper or stay an arm's length away from the art. In fact, this is where visitors come to view art, as well as make it.

The nonprofit visual arts organization is an affiliate of the N. C. Museum of Art, and since 1972, has sat on a 32-acre estate formerly owned by industrialist James G. Hanes.

Programs include exhibition openings; music, theater, and dance performances; fashion events; comedy; film screenings; art talks; and even cyclocross racing.

The setting also sets it apart. Many events are held outdoors, so visitors may enjoy a concert or film on an expansive lawn accented with boxwoods and wisteria trees.

SECCA also offers a variety of workshops, classes, and camps for adults, youth, and families.

Admission is free, though there may be a charge for some events, classes, or workshops.

750 Marguerite Dr., 336-725-1904, secca.org

FORM NEW PERSPECTIVES
THROUGH STORYTELLING

The name nails it. "MUSE," which is short for "museum," also stands for the Museum of Understanding Storytelling and Engagement.

This is a museum for the entire community. A history museum that emphasizes storytelling and dialogue. A space where people share their diverse stories so that others can learn and advance acceptance, understanding, and belonging.

A range of stories have been told through exhibits, public programs, and oral histories. They include the fight for Black voting rights, women's suffrage, and a film series that pairs street food cuisine with a film.

Events are designed to encourage dialogue and participation.

226 S Liberty St., 336-724-2842, musews.org

CELEBRATE AND HONOR
BLACK CULTURE AND HERITAGE

Considered the heart of the local Black community, the Delta Fine Arts Center is an art gallery, cultural center, and rental facility in East Winston-Salem.

It was founded in 1972 as a nonprofit by the Winston-Salem graduate chapter of Delta Sigma Theta Sorority, a national organization of Black college women founded in 1913.

Since then, the center has presented major exhibitions featuring some of the most influential Black artists in the country. Among its most popular are the biennial exhibitions, Invitational@DAC, and Raw Edges: Textile Art by Area African American Quilters.

The center acquired paintings and sculpture to enhance Winston-Salem State University's permanent collection and made significant donations to public collections in North Carolina. It also offers youth programs and virtual art and music lessons.

2611 New Walkertown Rd., 336-722-2625, deltaartscenter.org

EXPAND YOUR KNOWLEDGE
OF BLACK ART

Located on the campus Winston-Salem State University (an HBCU), the Diggs Gallery is known for having one of the South's leading collections of African and African American art.

The gallery offers one of the region's largest exhibition spaces dedicated to the arts of Africa and the African diaspora in North Carolina. For this, it's also been identified by the Smithsonian as one of the country's best regional facilities for exploring contemporary African art.

But this space isn't restricted to exhibitions. It's also an educational resource, producing publications and programs showcasing a broad range of artistic expression, with an emphasis on African American and regional art. Watch for announcements about the annual exhibition for the university's senior art majors.

The O'Kelly Library at Winston-Salem State University
601 S Martin Luther King Jr. Dr., 336-750-2458
wssu.edu/academics/colleges-and-departments/
college-of-arts-sciences-business-education/arts-humanities/diggs-gallery
wssu.edu/cg-okelly-library

FIND
AN ART-O-MAT

The crinkle of cellophane. The anticipation of not knowing exactly what you might get. And, of course, the retro super coolness of vintage cigarette machines repurposed to dispense original works of art by local artists. And at a price that's totally affordable—for $5, you can have an original piece of art. That's less than the price of a pack of cigarettes!

The appeal of the Art-o-mat never wanes. Since Art-o-mat creator Clark Whittington introduced the first one in a solo local art show in 1997, its following has only grown. The novelty has NOT worn off.

Now found in about 200 locations across the country, there are about 30 in the Winston-Salem area.

artomat.org

TAKE IN EVERYTHING
AT THE MILTON RHODES
CENTER FOR THE ARTS

Three theaters, two galleries, a school for visual arts, and a gift shop. Imagine all of this in a modern structure that was a textile mill more than a century ago.

Today, the Milton Rhodes Center for the Arts anchors the Arts Council of Winston-Salem & Forsyth County's Arts Campus. Two of its theaters are equipped with state-of-the-art lighting, projection and audio systems, configuration for theater-in-the-round productions, and fully retractable seating for non-theatrical events. The third smaller theater is a non-theatrical venue and provides a more participatory experience for audiences.

Don't miss the exhibits in the Main Gallery, as well as the Every Corner Gallery for juried works. Every Corner's unique location makes it an unusual venue to view art, but that's what makes it so special.

If you want to take some art home, peruse the Community Arts Gift Shop. Whether you're here for an event, performance, or lecture, be sure to add a little extra time to explore.

251 N Spruce St., 336-722-2585, intothearts.org

DELVE INTO GLOBAL CULTURES
AT THE LAM MUSEUM
OF ANTHROPOLOGY

A water container from Mali. Shell plaques from the Solomon Islands. Balinese offerings. These are a few examples of items you may find at the Lam Museum of Anthropology at Wake Forest University.

The museum holds archaeological artifacts, ethnographic objects, and visual arts of past and present peoples to inspire intercultural learning.

Learn about global cultures through its exhibits and educational programs both online and in person. Admission is free.

It also hosts free, themed open houses for families. These events usually offer craft projects, hands-on activities, music, and food. For a small fee, participants of all ages can engage in workshops that explore a culture through a related craft project.

Wake Forest University, Palmer Hall, Carroll Weathers Dr.
336-758-5282, lammuseum.wfu.edu

SUPPORT
BLACK THEATER

The North Carolina Black Repertory (NC Black Rep) Company, producers of the National Black Theatre Festival (NBTF), is the first professional Black theater company in North Carolina. It was founded by Larry Leon Hamlin in 1979, who also produced the first NBTF 10 years later.

NC Black Rep produces three to four seasonal mainstage productions and programs including the Teen Theatre Ensemble, a training program for young artists ages 13 to 19. Living Room Theatre is a reading series that produces staged readings of new works by nationally recognized playwrights throughout Winston-Salem. Locations for the series change from year to year.

419 N Spruce St., 336-723-2266, ncblackrep.org

WALK THROUGH THE DOORS
OF A HISTORIC WOMEN'S INSTITUTION

A stroll through the campus of Salem College is like walking through history. Its cobblestone streets and centuries old buildings makes one imagine what it must have been like in the days of early Moravian settlers.

The college, founded in 1772, is the oldest educational institution for girls and women in the US. The Single Sisters House, built in 1785, is the earliest building on campus.

The Single Sisters were unmarried women of the Moravian community and operated the school for many years. Their house is the longest standing building in the US that is continuously associated with the education of girls and women. It sheltered teachers and female students eager to learn mathematics, science, geography, the arts, and needlework.

The Single Sisters House was carefully restored in 2005 and includes the Single Sisters Museum, which is open to the public. It tells the story of the Single Sisters, their work to educate women, and the building in which they lived and taught.

601 S Church St., 336-721-2600, salem.edu

SPONSOR A SEAT
AT THE STAINED GLASS PLAYHOUSE

The Stained Glass Playhouse is a nonprofit community theater that presents affordable, professional-quality productions in an intimate setting.

Productions are held in the former sanctuary of Marvin United Methodist Church. Performances and events encompass moral messages, family values, and community issues. Past productions have included *Godspell*, *Dial M for Murder*, and *Our Town*.

For a tax-deductible donation, you can become a seat sponsor, which comes with a commemorative plaque permanently attached to a seat at the playhouse.

There are four productions annually: July/August, November, February, and May. Each production runs for three weekends, with shows on Friday and Saturday nights and a Sunday matinee.

4401 Indiana Ave., 336-661-4949, stainedglassplayhouse.org

HAVE A "MARVTASTIC" TIME
AT THE N. C. BLACK THEATRE FESTIVAL

Enjoy a taste of Broadway in Winston-Salem.

The biennial National Black Theatre Festival transforms the city into a mega performing arts center, with more than 130 performances in numerous venues over six days.

Created by the late Larry Leon Hamlin in 1989, the festival is produced by the N. C. Black Repertory Company, which he also founded. Hamlin coined the phrase "Marvtastic," which means there is nothing greater or better than.

It has attracted A-list celebrities such as Della Reese, John Amos, Oprah Winfrey, Ossie Davis, and Ruby Dee.

The festival kicks off with a star-studded celebrity opening night gala, and then continues with workshops, films, seminars, and a teen poetry slam.

Events held in multiple locations, 336-723-2266, nbtf.org

STUDY
EARLY SOUTHERN DECORATIVE ARTS

Within Old Salem Museum and Gardens sits an internationally recognized museum dedicated to the study of early Southern decorative arts.

Known as MESDA, the Museum of Early Southern Decorative Arts, it is the preeminent center for the research and study of Southern decorative arts and material culture.

MESDA researchers welcome enthusiasts, collectors, and the just plain curious. They invite you to broaden your own knowledge of early Southern decorative arts through an exclusive, two-hour Connoisseur Tour to learn more about MESDA's collections. Tours sell out fast, so book early and online.

924 S Main St., 336-721-7360, mesda.org

TIP

Research is at the core of what they do, so you can make an appointment for a virtual or in-person research session to explore your own personal decorative arts interests. The two-hour appointments are limited to four related individuals at a time and must be made at least seven days in advance. In addition, take a deeper dive into objects of a specific media, region, or time period with a collection study session.

PERCH ON A CHAIR
AT THE SUTTON CHAIR LIBRARY

A purple entry wall and a lipstick red sofa welcomes visitors to the Sutton Chair Library at Salem College.

Step inside and you'll be floored by the collection on display. The library houses 45 chairs considered iconic by historians and furniture designers. They range in structure, color, materials, and time periods.

What's super cool is how the chairs are displayed. They stand on custom shelving units with integrated lighting and cantilevered casework. A sophisticated lighting system and reflective surfaces create a museum-quality display. Some of the chairs are arranged on the dark reflective floors of the library, and others rest solo on their own shelves.

The library is a collaborative effort between the Sutton Initiative for Design Education (SIDE) and Salem College, and is located in the Robert E. Elberson Fine Arts Center. Students are invited to touch, sketch, photograph, study, and sit in the chairs.

Even if you don't give much thought to chairs, you'll probably want to take a few home with you.

412 Rams Dr., Salem College, chairlibrary.com

TIP
Anyone is welcome to visit the library at no cost. Call 336-721-2770 for an appointment.

RISE EARLY FOR AN EASTER SUNRISE SERVICE
AT GOD'S ACRE

The sacred Easter Sunrise Service at God's Acre is a more than 250-year tradition.

It's held at God's Acre, the Salem Congregation's graveyard, which has been described as hauntingly beautiful. The service draws thousands of people, both Moravian and non-Moravian. The silent procession to God's Acre begins around 6 a.m. in Salem Square. Salem Congregation is comprised of 12 Moravian churches and several of their bands play at various spots along the route.

The service begins as the sun starts its ascent over the graveyard. The feeling of reverence that overcomes you, knowing that you're part of a centuries old tradition, is indescribable.

Parking is at 720 Salt St., 235 S Church St., or 800 Old Salem Rd.
336-722-6504, salemcongregation.org/the-salem-moravian-graveyard-gods-acre

---

TIP
There are restrooms at various locations. Ushers are there to help guide worshippers. Pets aren't allowed because of graveyard regulations.

BONUS TIP

The Easter sunrise walk from Salem Square to God's acre is about a quarter of a mile but will take about a half-hour because of the crowd. Dress appropriately for the weather and wear walking shoes. Attire for the service is casual.

MEET AUTHORS, HEAR THEM SPEAK,
BUY THEIR BOOKS

World-renowned authors, emerging writers, and book lovers unite at the Festival of Books and Authors.

The festival takes place downtown over an entire weekend in late September. Events include a launch party, readings, author meet and greets, and a closing lecture. The festival is free, but books and some special events require a fee.

When the festival marked its 17th year in 2022, it had hosted more than 750 authors from around the world. Accolades for the festival's featured authors have included the Pulitzer Prize, the American Book Award and NEA, and MacArthur fellowships.

When it first began in 2004, it was the Bookmarks Book Festival. It's since grown to be the largest annual book festival in the Carolinas.

251 N Spruce St., 336-747-1471, bookmarksnc.org/festival

TRY TO FOLLOW
BLACK'S BRICK ROAD

While Industrialist tycoons R. J. Reynolds and P. H. Hanes developed and influenced Winston-Salem, it was George Black, the son of formerly enslaved people, who literally laid its foundation.

Black came to Winston-Salem in 1889 and learned the art of brickmaking at Hitchcock Brickyard. In 1920, he started making his own bricks by hand with Carolina red clay. His brickwork became much sought after and garnered prominent clients such as R. J. Reynolds.

His brickwork can be found throughout town, from the sidewalks of Old Salem to the mansions of Buena Vista and elsewhere.

Even after the process evolved and became mechanized, Black continued to handcraft thousands of bricks by hand daily behind his home. He lived there from 1934 until his death in 1980, and it's now on the National Register of Historic Places. You can still see stacks of bricks in the backyard.

For guided or personal tours, contact Triad Cultural Arts at charry@triadculturalarts.org.

111 Dellabrook Road, 336-757-8556, triadculturalarts.org

SHOPPING
AND FASHION

HUNT FOR SOMETHING
VINTAGE AND HANDMADE

Have you ever wondered what it would be like if Etsy were a brick-and-mortar store?

It's got to be similar to stepping into Design Archives Vintage and Handmade Emporium. It's the destination for a unique gift, addition to your closet, or accessory in your home.

Aptly named, this is where you're going to find a treasure trove of vintage upcycled and handmade jewelry, clothing, and accessories; whimsical handcrafts; vintage housewares; air plants; terrariums; small batch sauces; and other random oddities. It should be your very first stop if you're looking for a prom dress from the '80s, an ugly Christmas sweater, or vintage holiday ornaments.

It's also conveniently located near Foothills Brewpub and Footnotes Bookstore, so you can grab a bite and a pint or browse for books afterward.

636 W 4th Street, 336-602-2452, shopdesignarchives.com

GO TO REYNOLDA
FOR A LUXE DAY OUT

The charming historic buildings of Reynolda Village were once part of the 1,067-acre estate of the R. J. Reynolds family. It was modeled after an English village and included dairy barns, a cattle shed, school, post office, smokehouse, blacksmith shop, carriage house, and much more.

Today, they are transformed into upscale boutiques, restaurants, and services.

Retail offerings include fine custom jewelry, thoughtfully curated eyewear, upscale home furnishings and accessories, and designer fashions.

Whet your appetite with a sweet or savory crepe, steamed or pan-fried dumplings, or a made-to-order hot donut.

Whether you need stretching and toning, acupuncture, or a cut and color, knocking these off your to-do list at Reynolda Village feels luxurious.

2201 Reynolda Rd., 336-758-5584, rcynoldavillage.com

STOCK UP ON REGIONAL ITEMS AND VINTAGE CANDY
AT MAST GENERAL STORE

This is a one-stop shop for your retail dose of Southern charm, local items, and old-fashioned candy.

Mast General Store's roots date all the way back to 1883, when it began as the Taylor General Store. Through the years, its name evolved and its offerings expanded. It was said that a family could get whatever they needed at Mast—anything from cradles to caskets.

Today there are nine locations throughout the Carolinas, Virginia, and Tennessee. You can still find just about anything in a Mast General Store (but maybe not a casket). But if you're seeking a gift or souvenir that represents the region, check out the selection of handmade pottery, jewelry, and home decor. Mast devotees also stand by the quality of its shoes and outdoor apparel.

But the icing on this cake: all the candy you can imagine. Who remembers Dubble Bubble Gum Candy and Big League Chew (as in chewing tobacco) Bubble Gum? For all your string licorice, Cow Tales, and Laffy Taffy cravings—go to Mast.

516 N Trade St., 336-727-2015, mastgeneralstore.com

SEEK SOMETHING UNIQUE
AT PIEDMONT CRAFTSMEN

Whether it's a one-of-a-kind piece of statement jewelry, a vibrant scarf, or a smooth wooden fountain pen, you're bound to find something special at the Piedmont Craftsmen Gallery. It's even possible to find an affordable handmade work of art.

Whether you're shopping for yourself or someone else, a trip to the gallery is a treat in itself. The gallery is spacious and bright, with abundant natural light. A combination of gallery and store, Piedmont Craftsmen is also a nonprofit that offers classes and programs for the community. Patrons are encouraged to connect with its artists.

Shop in person at the gallery or online. If you shop online, you can have your gift delivered straight to its recipient along with a handwritten note, if requested.

601 N Trade St., 336-725-1516, piedmontcraftsmen.org

SOOTHE
YOUR BODY AND SOUL

Find skin care, aromatherapy, clothing, jewelry, books, and African art at this vibrant Trade Street boutique.

Sniff and sample an impressive array of Nubian Heritage shea butter soaps, body washes, and lotions, in addition to scented oils and incense.

A separate room holds books for all ages by local and Black authors. There's also a gallery of African masks, instruments, and other items imported or inspired by Africa. Racks hold colorful clothing, jewelry, and accessories from around the world.

But the real gem of this store is the customer service. Customers are greeted and treated as if they were guests in someone's home. Whether you buy anything or not, you leave feeling a little lighter and kinder for the warm exchange and positive affirmations shared.

545 N Trade St., Ste. 1H, 336-723-7685, bodyandsoulncstore.com

HEAD TO THE FAIRGROUNDS
FOR FRESH MEATS, PRODUCE, AND MORE!

The Carolina Classic Fair is just once a year, but the Fairgrounds Farmers Market lures you back throughout the year for fresh meats, produce, baked goods, and homemade jams and jellies.

The indoor, year-round market also hosts special exhibits, such as the craft fair, and competitions like the Berry Fresh Pie or Saucy Salsa contests.

Supporting the Fairgrounds Farmers Market also ensures a longstanding tradition can continue. In operation since 1974, it is Forsyth County's longest-running source for locally raised fruits, vegetables, and proteins. That's right, this farmers market is an original. Long before farm-to-fork and organic farming became mainstream, the farmers, ranchers, and growers at this market were simply continuing a tradition of sustaining their own families with what they could grow or raise. These are seasoned farmers with many decades of lessons to share and stories to tell. They are as much a draw as what they sell.

2532 Farmers Market Way, 336-727-2236, wsfairgrounds.com/farmersmarket

SHOP SUSTAINABLY
AT COBBLESTONE FARMERS MARKET

You know what to expect from most farmers markets: fruits and veggies; organic, free-range dairy, beef, pork, and poultry products; and sometimes fresh seafood from the coast.

Then there are markets that offer a little more. Cobblestone Farmers Market is one of them—and it's open year-round. Take the time to wander the cobblestone street of this charming downtown farmers market and you might find fresh fermented krauts, kimchis, and beverages; award-winning goat cheese and extraordinary healthy snacks; nutrient-dense, freshly foraged mushrooms; and handcrafted, ethically sourced tempeh.

There's so much more. This is the spot to pick up what you need for the week or the weekend, grab a hostess gift, or party favor.

You can also feel good about supporting local farmers, growers, and makers. Products are fully vetted and producers must adhere to sustainable, naturally grown, and humane practices.

1007 S Marshall St., 336-721-7300, thecobblestonefarmersmarket.com

TIPS
Pets aren't permitted.
Preorder pickup is available onsite.
SNAP/EBT, WIC, and Senior FMNP
SNAP/EBT accepted.

CRAFT
A HANDMADE HOLIDAY LIST

Make a holiday shopping list that's filled with handcrafted gifts made by skilled artisans. Then knock out that list at the Piedmont Craftsmen's Fair.

The annual fair, held at the Benton Convention Center in November, draws more than a hundred of the finest makers in the Southeast. Their inventory includes unique home goods, jewelry, ceramics, glass, textiles, furniture, and decor.

In addition, there are live demonstrations and mix and mingles with the makers, making this more than a shopping opportunity. You get to know the artists and hear what motivates and inspires them. You can watch them at work and witness their passion for their craft. This is what makes you feel a connection to what they've made. So the next time you use, wear, or look at what they've created, you'll recall the hands that made it and the heart behind it.

Benton Convention Center
301 W 5th St., 336-725-1516, piedmontcraftsmen.org/fair

ACTIVITIES
BY SEASON

SPRING

Stroll around Town, 64

Live the Lake Life at Salem Lake, 66

Soak In the Views at the Quarry, 67

Picnic by a Secret Waterfall, 70

Shop Sustainably at Cobblestone Farmers Market, 124

Rise Early for an Easter Sunrise Service at God's Acre, 112

Wander Reynolda Museum, Historic House, and Gardens, 84

Eat, Dance, and Shop at the Greek Festival, 44

SUMMER

Dance and Sway the Night Away at the Downtown Summer Music Series, 47

Watch a Film under the Stars at Reynolda, 48

Chill Out at the Big Chill Fundraiser, 49

Rock Out in the Coal Pit, 53

Cheer for the Dash and the Disco Turkeys, 60

Get Loud at the Madhouse, 62

Stand at the Site of the Nation's First Fourth of July Celebration, 81

Score Some World-Class Tennis, 61

• •

FALL

Gear Up for Cycle Racing and Live Music, 50

Meet Authors, Hear Them Speak, Buy Their Books, 114

Kick Off Fall with a Classic, 51

Taste and Dance Your Way through Latin America, 52

Walk with the Deacons, Groove to the Red Sea of Sound, 63

Get Spooked with a Haunted Tour of Winston-Salem, 82

WINTER

Feel the Holiday Magic at Tanglewood, 54

Hear the Oldest Continuous Mixed Wind Ensemble in the Nation, 45

Ride through Old Salem in a Horse-Drawn Carriage, 93

Hit the Moravian Culinary Trail, Starting at Salem Kitchen, 2

Craft a Handmade Holiday List, 126

Follow Native Root for Indigenous Cuisine, 22

Pause, Learn, and Reflect: Experience Black History, 91

Celebrate and Honor Black Culture and Heritage, 99

• •

SUGGESTED
ITINERARIES

FAMILY FUN

Get Loud at the Madhouse, 62

Hang Out at the Art Park, 56

Have Fun While Learning at Kaleidium, 43

Soak In the Views at the Quarry, 67

Chill Out at the Big Chill Fundraiser, 49

Live the Lake Life at Salem Lake, 66

Cheer for the Dash and the Disco Turkeys, 60

Stroll around Town, 64

Watch a Film under the Stars at Reynolda, 48

Ride a Dinosaur, 65

HISTORY BUFFS

Dig into History at Bethabara Park, 86

Stand at the Site of the Nation's First Fourth of July Celebration, 81

Spend a Day at Old Salem Museum and Gardens, 74

Pause, Learn, and Reflect: Experience Black History, 91

Wander Reynolda Museum, Historic House, and Gardens, 84

Try to Follow Black's Brick Road, 115

Sit in a One-Room Schoolhouse, 90

Celebrate and Honor Black Culture and Heritage, 99

Get Spooked with a Haunted Tour of Winston-Salem, 82

Form New Perspectives through Storytelling, 98

• •

NIGHT OUT

Broaden Your Film Horizons at a/perture cinema, 41

Turn Date Night into Play Night at ROAR, 37

Gather, Listen, and Create at Industry Hill, 40

Drink In the Town with a Craft Draft Crawl, 4

Sample North Carolina Craft Beers and Wines, 10

Sign Up for Sunday School at Ginger Fox Beverage, 8

Play like a Kid at the Kimpton Cardinal, 42

Indulge at the (Chocolate) Bar, 13

Recapture Your Youth at a Neighborhood Bar, 27

Meet Friends after Work at the Library Bar, 31

ARTS AND CULTURE

Celebrate and Honor Black Culture and Heritage, 99

Binge on Films at RiverRun International Film Festival, 46

Immerse Yourself in Books at Bookmarks, 95

Find an Art-O-Mat, 101

Wander Reynolda Museum, Historic House, and Gardens, 84

Form New Perspectives through Storytelling, 98

Expand Your Knowledge of Black Art, 100

Delve into Global Cultures at the Lam Museum of Anthropology, 103

• •

BLACK HISTORY AND CULTURE

Pause, Learn, and Reflect: Experience Black History, 91

Have a "Marvtastic" Time at the N. C. Black Theatre Festival, 107

Form New Perspectives through Storytelling, 98

Try to Follow Black's Brick Road, 115

Celebrate and Honor Black Culture and Heritage, 99

Sit in a One-Room Schoolhouse, 90

Support Black Theater, 104

Expand Your Knowledge of Black Art, 100

Walk with the Deacons, Groove to the Red Sea of Sound, 63

SUPPORT BLACK-OWNED BUSINESSES

Sample North Carolina Craft Beers and Wines, 10

Revive Your Soul with Food, 28

Make Friends and Forge Relationships
  over Fried Green Tomatoes and Okra, 19

Relish Coastal Flavors without Driving to the Beach, 21

Soothe Your Body and Soul, 122

INDEX

6th and Vine, 76

A. H. Bahnson House, 31

African American history, 91, 99, 100

a/perture cinema, 41

Arcade Airbnb, 38

Arcade games, 26, 38, 83

Archaeology, 86, 103

Art, 4–5, 7, 10, 19, 28, 40, 41, 42, 43, 46, 48, 51, 56–57, 75, 76–77, 84, 91, 92, 94, 95, 97, 99, 100, 101, 102, 103, 104, 105, 107, 108–109, 110, 115, 121, 122, 126

ARTivity on the Green, 56

Art-o-mat, 101

Arts District, 4–5, 19, 76

Artworks Gallery, 76–77

B. L. L. Rotisserie Factory, 29

Bailey Park, 39, 46, 50, 64

Bakeries, 3, 6–7, 74, 93

Barbecue, 24, 26, 30

Bars, 4–5, 8–9, 27, 31, 42, 48, 88–89

Baseball, 60

Beer, 4–5, 10, 26, 27, 37, 40, 49, 60, 88–89, 95

Bethabara Park, 86

Big Chill, 49

Black, George, 115

Black art, 99, 100

Black history, 74, 91

Black Mountain Chocolate Bar, 13

Black's bricks, 115

Bobby Boy Bakeshop, 7

Body and Soul, 122

Bookmarks, 32, 95, 114

Bowman Gray Stadium, 62

Bread, 6–7, 22, 74

Breathing Room, The, 88–89

C. G. Memorial Park, 69

Café Arthur's, 23

Camel City Barbecue Factory, 26

Camino Bakery, 7

Candy, 120

Carolina Classic Fair, 51, 123

Carolina Disco Turkeys, 60

Carolina History and Haunts, 82

Carolina Vineyards and Hops, 10

Childress, Richard, 62

Chocolate, 4, 13, 55

Cinema Under the Stars, 48

Coalpit Live, 5, 53

Cobblestone Farmers Market, 124

Cocktails, 8, 13, 31, 32, 95

Coffee, 7, 23, 31, 32, 53, 65, 79, 95

Craft Draft Crawl, 4

Cycling, 50

Demon Deacons, 63

Delta Fine Arts Center, 99

Delurk Gallery, 76–77

• •

Design Archives, 118

Dewey's Bakery, 3

Diggs Gallery, 100

Dinosaur Playground, 65

Donuts/doughnuts, 12, 18, 44, 119

Dough-Joe's Coffee and Doughnuts, 18

Downtown Arts District Association, 76

Downtown Summer Music Series, 47

Easter Sunrise Service, 2, 112

Eastern Standard, 9

Eight Points Muay Thai, 88–89

Fair Witness, 9

Fairgrounds Farmers Market, 123

Farmers Markets, 22, 123, 124

Festival of Books and Authors, 114

Festival of Lights, 54–55

Fiesta, 52

Film screenings, 92, 97

First Fourth of July Celebration, 81

First Friday Gallery Hop, 76

Football, 63

Footnote Coffee & Cocktails, 32, 95

Forsyth Seafood Market & Cafe, 21

Galleries, 76–77, 84, 91, 92, 97, 99, 100, 102, 121, 122

Gears and Guitars Festival, 50

Gifted Gallery2, 76–77

Ginger Fox Beverage, 8

God's Acre, 2, 112–113

Graylyn Estate, 80

Greek Festival, 44

Greek food, 44

Hamlin, Larry Leon, 104, 107

Haunted Tour, 82

Heritage Carriages, 93

Hispanic League, 52

Holidays, 2, 45, 54–55, 93, 118, 126

Honky Tonk Smokehouse, 26

Hoots Roller Bar & Beer Co., 4, 88–89

Horse-drawn carriage ride, 55, 93

Horticulture Lab, 96

Hot Dog City, 24–25

Hot dogs, 15, 24–25, 60

Ice cream, 49, 80

Indigenous food, 22

Industry Hill, 5, 40, 49

Innovation Quarter, 13, 36, 64

Italian food, 20, 29, 87

Katharine Brasserie & Bar, 42

Kimpton Cardinal Hotel, 56

Joymongers Barrel Hall, 5

Joyner's Bar, 9

Kaleidium, 43

Kermit's Hot Dog House, 24–25

Krankie's Coffee, 32

Krispy Kreme, 12, 18, 44, 51

La Botana, 16

Lam Museum of Anthropology, 103

Lesser-Known Beer Co., 5

Library Bar, 31

Long Branch Trail, 64

Louie and Honey's Kitchen, 7

Madhouse, 62

Mast General Store, 120

Mexican food, 16, 37, 52

Milton Rhodes Center for the Arts, 102

Mission Pizza, 20

Mixxer, 40

Monstercade, 27

Moravian chicken pie, 2

Moravian cookies, 2–3, 74, 93

Moravian Culinary Trail, 2

Moravian sugar cake, 2

Moravians, 2, 45, 74, 79, 81, 87, 96, 105, 112

Mozelle's, 17

Mr. Barbecue, 26

Mrs. Hanes' Moravian Cookies, 3

Museum of Early Southern Decorative Arts (MESDA), 75, 108

Museum of Understanding Storytelling and Engagement (MUSE), 98

Museums, 43, 48, 74–75, 83, 84, 90, 97, 98, 103, 105, 108

N. C. Black Theatre Festival, 107

N. C. Black Repertory Company, 107

NASCAR, 62, 83

National Register of Historic Places, 78, 84, 87, 115

Native Root, 22

North Trade Street Arts Center, 76–77

Oak Grove School, 90

Old Salem, 3, 64, 74, 79, 86, 93, 96, 108, 115

• •

Old Salem Coffee Pot, 79

Old Salem Museum and Gardens, 74, 108

Outdoor concerts, 2, 39, 45, 47, 50, 97

P. B.'s Takeout, 24–25

Petty, Richard, 62

Piedmont Aviation Snack Bar, 15

Piedmont Craftsmen Gallery, 76–77, 121

Piedmont Craftsmen's Fair, 126

Piedmont Quarry, 67

Pizza, 20, 29

Porch Kitchen & Cantina, 88–89

Pulliam's, 24

Quarry at Grant Park, The, 67

Radar Brewing Company, 5, 40

Ramkat, The, 40

Red Sea of Sound, 63

Reynolda House, 48, 84

Reynolda Village, 18, 70–71, 119

Reynolds, R. J., 5, 42, 53, 56, 82, 83, 84, 115, 119

RiverRun International Film Festival, 46

ROAR, 37

Rotisserie chicken, 29

Salem Band, 45

Salem College, 2, 10, 105, 110

Salem Lake, 64, 66

Salem Square, 2, 45, 81, 112–113

Salem Town Hall, 87

Sawtooth School for Visual Art, 94

Sawtooth Shop, 94

• •

Sayso Coffee, 32

Sculpture Park, 56

Seafood, 21, 37, 124

Seed-Saving Lab, 96

Shell Oil clamshell station, 78

Sherwood, The, 30

Silver Moon Saloon, 76–77

Single Brothers, 9, 76–77

Single Brothers Garden, 96

Single Sisters House, 105

Small Batch Beer Co., 5

Social club, 37

Soul food, 28

Southeastern Center for Contemporary Art (SECCA), 46, 97

Spring House Restaurant, 31

Stained Glass Playhouse, 106

Strollway Pedestrian Bridge, 64

Studio 7, 76–77

Sutler's, 11

Sutton Chair Library, 110

Sutton Initiative for Design Education (SIDE), 110

Sweet Potatoes restaurant, 19, 76–77

Swaim's Grocery, 27

Tanglewood, 54

Taste of the Triad Restaurant, 28

Thai food, 14

Thai Sawatdee, 14

Tennis, 61

Tomato pie, 17

• •

Trade Street, 4, 9, 19, 20, 76–77, 120, 121, 122

Triad Cultural Arts African American Heritage Tour, 91

Vintage shopping, 118, 120

Visual Index, 76–77

Wake Forest football, 63

Wake Forest University, 36, 61, 63, 80, 103

Waterfalls, 43, 70

West End Mill Works, 11, 88

West Salem Art Hotel, 92

Wilkerson Moravian Bakery, 3

Winkler's Bakery, 3, 74, 93

Winston Cup Museum, 83

Winston-Salem Dash, 60

Winston-Salem Open, 61

Winston-Salem State University, 63, 99, 100

Wise Man Brewing, 5, 40